Competition Law

Competition Law

J. H. Agnew

Humberside College of Higher Education, Hull

London
ALLEN & UNWIN
Boston   Sydney

Allen & Unwin (Publishers) Ltd,
40 Museum Street, London WC1A 1LU, UK

Allen & Unwin (Publishers) Ltd,
Park Lane, Hemel Hempstead, Herts HP2 4TE, UK

Allen & Unwin Inc.,
8 Winchester Place, Winchester, Mass. 01890, USA

Allen & Unwin (Australia) Ltd,
8 Napier Street, North Sydney, NSW 2060, Australia

First published in 1985

British Library Cataloguing in Publication Data

Agnew, J. H.
  Competition law.
1. Antitrust law—European Economic Community
countries
I. Title
341.7′53   [LAW]
ISBN 0–04–343002–3
ISBN 0–04–343003–1 Pbk

Library of Congress Cataloging in Publication Data

Agnew, J. H. (John Hardman)
  Competition law.
Bibliography: p.
Includes index.
1. Antitrust law—European Economic Community
countries. I. Title.
LAW   343.4′072   85–11165
LAW   344.0372
ISBN 0–04–343002–3 (alk. paper)
ISBN 0–04–343003–1 (pbk.: alk. paper)

Set in 11 on 12 point Times by Grove Graphics, Tring,
and printed in Great Britain by Billing and Sons Ltd,
London and Worcester

Contents

Preface

In recent years, there has been a rapid growth in the amount of legislation with the object of securing a more competitive business environment. Competition, or anti-trust, law has thus assumed a more prominent place as an area of study on business and management courses. Unnecessary costs can be avoided by business if the effects of laws relating to competition are taken account of when business contracts, and other business transactions and practices are being considered.

Competition law lies at the crossroads between economics and law, and is, in many respects, a direct implementation of economic and social policy. It is therefore not possible to fully understand the law in this area without some background in the theories of competition and monopoly. This book therefore includes an introductory chapter on these economic theories, and an attempt has been made throughout the book to examine the law from the basis of these theories. The book is not intended to be a full treatise on competition law, being an introductory study aimed primarily at students taking business degrees and diplomas. It is also hoped that it will be of value to students on law degrees, particularly those taking business and European law options; businessmen who require some knowledge as to how their organizations may be affected by the competition rules; and to lawyers who are not experts in the field of competition.

I wish to record my appreciation and thanks to Mr Howard Davies, Head of School of Finance, Humberside College of Higher Education, not only for his chapter on economic theories, but also for his general encouragement, and for his assistance in the preparation of the remainder of the book, particularly in relation to the economic content. I take full responsibility, however, for any errors or omissions.

I also wish to express my thanks to Mrs Patricia Holmes, who not only typed the manuscript, but was also very helpful in its preparation. No book can be published without the hard work of secretaries. Thanks, too, to the Publishers for their help in the production of this book.

John Agnew
Hull, September 1984

Table of Statutes

Common Market

United States

Table of Cases

1

An Overview
of Competition Law

Rationale of competition law

The fundamental rationale of competition law lies in the
proposition that competition yields social benefits which are
lost through monopoly, and that legal controls can reduce, or
even eliminate, the damage done. The welfare of a society
which establishes an effective form of regulation will thereby
improve. This proposition raises a number of complex
problems which require some answers if competition law is to
be evaluated and understood. These questions are:

(1) What precisely is meant by the terms 'competition' and
    'monopoly'?
(2) What is the nature of the social damage caused by
    monopoly power?
(3) What is the extent of that damage?
(4) To what extent can legal regulation reduce that damage
    in principle? and
(5) To what extent does the actual system of competition
    law in the United Kingdom confer the benefits available
    in principle?

Before these questions are discussed it is both desirable and
useful to begin with a general survey of competition law in
order to provide an overview of the subject.

Historical background

Although modern competition legislation only dates back to 1948 with the passing of the Monopolies and Restrictive Practices (Inquiry and Control) Act, laws to control monopoly and economic power date back many centuries. The contribution made by the common law, and in particular the concepts of restraint of trade, conspiracy and the public interest, to the development of competition law should not be overlooked.

Two reasons accounted for the interest of the law in monopoly. In the first place, trade was generally local in character, and it was therefore relatively easy to achieve a monopoly. This was reinforced in many trades by the guild system, as to practice a particular trade in a town, a person would have to belong to the appropriate guild and abide by its rules. Secondly, the grant of a monopoly was an important revenue raiser for the monarch, who therefore found it desirable to forbid private monopolies and declare them illegal.

With the rapid growth of trade, and a mercantile class in the sixteenth century, coupled with the declining power of the royal prerogative, the right of the monarch to confer monopolies was increasingly called into question. In *Darcy v Allen (1602)* the common law disapproved of this power. The case concerned the grant of a monopoly to a manufacturer of playing cards, who was claiming damages for an infringement of his sole rights. The grant was held void, and he thus lost his claim for damages.

The monarch continued to grant monopolies, in spite of this case and the Statute of Monopolies passed in 1642, which declared all monopolies to be void except for patents and new inventions. It was not until 1689 that the Bill of Rights finally ended the grant of royal monopolies. As a result of this, and as the growth of trade and the improvement in communications made it much more difficult for traders to monopolize the market, the law lost interest in monopoly control. It turned its attention instead to restrictive trading agreements, which were becoming more common as traders recognized the advantages to themselves of restricting competition between them. The Courts thus started to develop the doctrine of restraint of trade.

Restraint of trade

A contract in restraint of trade was judicially defined by Lord Diplock in *Petrofina (Great Britain) Ltd. v Martin (1966)* as:

> . . . one in which a party (the covenantor) agrees with any other party (the covenantee) to restrict his liberty in the future to carry on trade with any other person not parties to the contract in such manner as he chooses.

The law has recognized three kinds of restraint of trade. These are:

(1) restraints between the vendor and purchaser of a business whereby the vendor covenants not to compete against the purchaser;
(2) restraints between employer and employee, whereby the employee covenants not to work in competition to his employer, even after he has ceased to be an employee; and
(3) restraints accepted by businessmen aimed at restricting or preventing competition between them.

Competition law is, of course, primarily concerned with the third category of restraints, but it is in dealing with the first two that the Courts have established the principles upon which the modern law of competition is based.

This doctrine of restraint of trade developed during the era when *laissez-faire*, and its legal counterpart, freedom of contract, were in vogue. And it is here that there is a conflict inherent in the restraint of trade doctrine − that between freedom of contract and freedom of trade. The idea behind freedom of contract is that a person can freely enter into any contract he wishes, and on what terms he wishes, subject only to the agreement of the other party to the contract. Freedom of trade allows a person to trade free from any restrictions. This conflict has arisen because people have used their right to contract freely in order to restrict their right to trade freely. The conflict has been partially resolved by the law holding that while restraints of trade are generally void as being against public policy, they may be allowed in certain circumstances, that is if they are reasonable and not contrary to the public interest.

The modern doctrine was established in *Nordenfelt v Maxim Nordenfelt Guns and Ammunition Co. (1894)*. This case involved an undertaking given by the seller of a business that he would for a period of 25 years, and anywhere in the world, refrain from setting up in business in competition with the purchaser. Lord McNaghten stated in his judgement;

> . . . all restraints of trade in themselves, if there is nothing more are void. That is the general rule. But there are exceptions; restraints of trade and interference with individual liberty of action may be justified by the special circumstances of a particular case. It is sufficient justification, and, indeed, it is the only justification if the restriction is reasonable — reasonable that is in reference to the interests of the parties concerned and reasonable in reference to the interests of the public . . .

Thus the *Nordenfelt* case established at common law that all restraints of trade are void unless it can be shown that:

(1) the restraint is reasonable as between the parties to the agreement, that is that it goes no further than is necessary to protect one of the parties from the unreasonable competition of the other; and

(2) the restraint is not unreasonably damaging to the public interest.

Its significance as a doctrine is that the concept of the public interest has become an integral part of the legislation which now govern monopolies and restrictive trading agreements.

Very few cases have been concerned, however, with restrictive trading agreements, but have been concerned primarily with restraints imposed upon the seller of a business, and on an employee. One of the few cases to come before the courts, until the petrol solus agreement cases of the late 1960s was *McEllistrim v Ballymacelligot Co-op,*

Agricultural and Dairy Society (1919). Under an agreement all members of the Society (and if a producer was not a member of the Society he would have great difficulty in finding a market as the agreement operated over a wide area) were required to sell their produce to it. If a member wished to opt out he was required to sell his shares, and this could only be done with the Society's permission. The agreement was declared void as being an unreasonable restraint of trade. The rules went further than was necessary in order to protect the interest of the Society, which was stated to be ensuring stability in the market.

The restraint of trade doctrine has, in recent years, been applied to petrol solus agreements, whereby the owner of a garage agrees to take all his supplies from one petrol company. In *Petrofina (Great Britain) Ltd. v Martin*, such an agreement was held to be an unreasonable restraint of trade. This case was followed by *Esso Petroleum Co. Ltd. v Harper's Garage (Stourport) Ltd. (1968)*, where there were two agreements restraining the defendant from obtaining supplies from elsewhere – one for 4 years and 5 months, and one for 21 years, contained in mortgages irredeemable for those periods. The House of Lords held the longer contract to be in restraint of trade because it was unreasonable and contrary to the public interest. They enforced the shorter contract, however, as being a reasonable period to protect the interests of the plaintiff.

Before the restraint of trade doctrine can apply, a person's freedom to trade must be restricted. If, therefore, prior to making an agreement, there is not right to trade, the doctrine cannot apply. As Lord Reid put it in the *Harper's Garage* case:

Restraint of trade appears to me to imply that a man contracts to give up some freedom which otherwise he would have had. A person buying or leasing land had no previous right to be there at all, let alone to trade there, and when he takes possession of that land subject to a negative restrictive covenant he gives up no right or freedom which he previously had. . . . In the present case the respondents before they made this agreement were entitled to use this land in any lawful way they chose, and by making this agreement they had agreed to restrict their right by giving up their right to sell there petrol not supplied by the appellants.

This seems to imply, that if the constraints are contained in a mortgage used to buy the land, the contract, even for the longer period, would have been upheld.

The greatest weakness in the restraint of trade doctrine preventing business practices which restrict competition is that the restrictive covenant is not illegal, but merely void as being contrary to public policy, and therefore unenforceable as between the parties. The only occasion on which the matter would come before the courts is if one of the parties breaks the covenant, and is therefore being sued for breach of contract. It does not give the right to third parties to take legal action because they are adversely affected by the restriction. So, if a manufacturer gives sole distributor rights to a dealer, in return for that dealer not selling the products of other manufacturers, even if this contract is in restraint of trade at common law, other dealers or manufacturers who may be damaged by the contract cannot take any legal action under this doctrine. As long as the parties to a contract which is in restraint of trade keep to it, the law is powerless to intervene.

Conspiracy

This weakness in the doctrine of restraint of trade led a trader, who had suffered loss as a result of collective action by other traders, to seek an alternative line of attack. This was the tort of conspiracy. Conspiracy was defined in *Muleakey v R (1868)* as 'an agreement of two or more to do an unlawful act, or to do a lawful act by unlawful means', and such a conspiracy is a tort if it causes loss to the plaintiff. The basis of the tort of conspiracy is, therefore, collusive action which results in some loss or damage to the interests of a third person. The cases show, however, that a trader who is injured in this way has little chance of succeeding under this tort.

The issue arose in *Mogul Steamship Co. Ltd. v McGregor, Gow & Co. (1892)*. A number of shipping companies combined together to form an Association to regulate shipping services between China and the United Kingdom. They made agreements as to the division of cargoes, the prices to be charged and offered discounts to shippers who dealt exclusively with members of the Association. They also reduced their freights whenever competition threatened. An outsider found that in order to compete with the Association he had to run his business at a loss. He sued, claiming that the members of the Association were party to an unlawful combination, and their actions consequently illegal. The House of Lords held that the Association were acting in order to protect their own interests, and not to damage the interests of the appellant. An outsider thus injured by a combination will have to show that as well as suffering injury, the predominant motive of the combination is to injure him and not to protect the interests of the combination, unless unlawful means are used.

Similar issues arose in *Sorrell v Smith* and *Ware and de Freville v Motor Trades Association*. In *Sorrell v Smith (1925)*, a new newsagents shop was opened in an area without permission of the local newsagents trade association. The association procured Sorrell, one of their members, to obtain his supplies from another wholesaler, and not the one who supplied the new newsagent. At the request of this wholesaler, the newspaper proprietors intervened, and threatened to refuse to supply the first wholesaler unless he refused to supply Sorrell. Sorrell sought an injunction to restrain the defendants from interfering with his business with that wholesaler. Sorrell lost his claim. Viscount Cave summed up the law thus:

(1) A combination of two or more persons wilfully to injure a man in his trade is unlawful.

(2) If the real purpose of the combination is not to injure another, but to forward or defend the trade of those who enter into it, then no wrong is committed.

Ware and de Freville v Motor Trades Association (1921) involved the enforcement of resale price maintenance by collective action. If any distributor sold at a price below that laid down by the motor manufacturers he would be put on a stop list and no member of the Association would supply him. If any did, then they would also be put on the stop list. The Court of Appeal held that this practice of the Motor Trade Association was neither a conspiracy to do an unlawful act, nor to do a lawful act by unlawful means. The Association was merely acting in the best interests of its members, and that was the main motive of the combination. The principle in this decision was approved by the House of Lords in *Thorn v Motor Trades Association (1937)*.

Under common law the position was, and indeed still is, that a combination in undue restraint of trade does not give the right to a person who is injured by the combination to seek damages or an injunction, unless that person can show that the predominant motive of the combination was to cause harm to him. If the main aim was the mutual protection of the members of the combination and intended to further their own interests, even at the expense of the interests of others, then no right of action accrued, unless unlawful means were used. The only real sanction at common law to restrain restrictive and anti-competitive practices is that the contract is void, and thus unenforceable, unless the contract is reasonable. But those who enter into contracts in their own interests are likely to keep to them, and if so, the common law is powerless to intervene.

Modern legislation

The early part of the twentieth century, particularly the inter-war period, saw a great increase in the concentration of economic power and cartels, which had the effect of restraining competition. This process was often encouraged by government in the periods of recession at that time. In the 1940s, these restraints of competition, in particular price cartels and abuses of monopoly or dominant situations, were thought to be in many instances injurious to the public interest, and one of the reasons for the relatively poor performance of British industry.

The *White Paper on Employment Policy* (1944) in considering competition restraints stated:

> There has in recent years been a growing tendency towards combines and towards agreements . . . by which manufacturers have sought to control prices and output, divide markets, and fix conditions of sale . . . . The Government will therefore seek power to inform them-

selves of the extent and effect of restrictive agreements and the activities of combines; and to take appropriate action to check practices which may bring advantages to the sectional producing interests, but work to the detriment of the country as a whole.

The *Monopolies and Restrictive Practices (Inquiry and Control) Act* (1948), which followed the White Paper was very limited in scope. It set up the Monopolies and Restrictive Practices Commission (MRPC) (now the Monopoly and Mergers Commission – MMC), which was charged with examining, when asked to do so by the secretary of state, cartels and the activities of dominant firms where a monopoly situation (defined as one-third of the relevant market) existed, and to report on whether the activities of these firms operated against the public interest.

The Act did not condemn concentrations of economic power as such, but merely brought them under some form of control. As Borrie (1980) says, the Act adopted a neutral and empirical approach, and there was no presumption as to the acceptability or otherwise of particular practices. This approach still largely exists in United Kingdom competition law and policy with certain exceptions.

Since 1948 there have been numerous other statutes which have extended competition control, and the 1948 Act itself has been repealed and replaced by other legislation. In particular, the Fair Trading Act, 1973, created the office of the Director General of Fair Trading, one of whose principal roles is to oversee competition policy. The United Kingdom, as a member of the European Economic Community, is also subject to the competition law and policies of the Common Market. Although EEC law is part of domestic national law, United Kingdom law will be taken to mean law having its source in the United Kingdom parliament and courts, while Common Market law will be taken to mean law having its origins in the EEC Treaty.

It is possible to classify competition law into three distinct categories, though there is some overlap, and this book will follow this classification. In the first place, legislation provides for control over the activities of a single firm which is in a monopoly or dominant position, or which possesses some degree of market power. Secondly, there is the power to exercise control over merger situations. The final category is concerned with restrictive trading agreements.

Monopoly and dominant positions

Under the Fair Trading Act, the Director has the discretionary power to refer to the MMC any suspected monopoly situation, defined as at least 25 per cent of the relevant market, in the supply or acquisition of goods and services in, or the export of goods from, the United Kingdom. Monopoly situations can be structural, that is that one firm accounts for the 25 per cent market share, or behavioural or complex, where two or more firms, who together have a 25 per cent share of the market so conduct their affairs as to restrict competition between them, a typical oligopoly situation.

It must be stressed that United Kingdom law does not condemn a monopoly situation in itself. Before action can be taken against a monopoly it must be established by the MMC that a monopoly situation is operating against the public interest. Where the MMC so concludes, it may make recommendations for action to the secretary of state, who has various powers to make orders enforcing these recommendations, including the prohibition of certain practices, control of prices and even disinvestment. The more normal course of events would be for the secretary of state to request the Director to obtain an undertaking from the firm concerned.

Monopoly practices which have attracted criticism in MMC investigations have included charging too high prices, discriminatory and predatory pricing, and various other practices which restrain competition, including, in the Household Detergents reference, high advertising costs. In the main, the MMC has been particularly critical of firms in a monopoly situation who engage in practices which erect barriers to other firms entering the market.

As well as the control laid down in the Fair Trading Act, monopolies also come under the EEC controls, though the term 'dominant position' is used rather than monopoly. Whether a firm is in a dominant position is a question of fact to be decided in each case, and not a question of a particular market share. The EEC Treaty, Article 86, provides that any abuse of a dominant position within the Common Market shall be prohibited if it effects trade between Member States. As with monopoly control under United Kingdom legislation, it is not the dominant position itself which is condemned, but its abuse.

There are important differences of approach between the United Kingdom and Common Market control of dominant situations. The Common Market rules prohibit certain conduct in the rules themselves and penal sanctions can be applied for their breach. The United Kingdom law only provides for the prohibition of conduct by firms in a dominant situation after an investigation by the Monopolies Commission, and penalties can be imposed only for breach of a court order.

Certain anti-competitive practices by a single firm, whether or not carried out by firms who are in a monopoly situation or in a dominant market position, can be investigated by the Director and referred to the MMC under the powers given in the Competition Act, 1980. These are practices which have the effect of restricting, preventing, or distorting competition. However, although a firm does not need to be in a monopoly or dominant position, it is unlikely that a competition reference will be made unless the firm concerned possesses some degree of market power. The procedure laid down in the Act follows closely the monopoly reference procedure, but it does provide for a simpler and quicker investigation, and is likely to be used instead of a monopoly investigation in many instances.

Merger control

Control over mergers was first established in 1965, and now comes under the Fair Trading Act. Mergers can be referred for an investigation by the MMC in two instances. First where, as a result of the merger, a monopoly situation would be created or enhanced, or secondly where the assets to be taken over exceed £15 million. The inclusion of the asset value criterion allows vertical and diversified, as well as horizontal mergers to be referred for investigation. The power to refer lies not with the Director, but only with the secretary of state, though the Director is under a duty to advise him.

The MMC must report on whether the merger operates or may operate against the public interest, in which case the secretary of state has the power to prevent it, or if it has taken place, to order a demerger, though this latter power has never been used. In the majority of cases where the MMC has condemned a proposed merger, undertakings are usually accepted by the Director not to proceed with the proposal.

Restrictive trade practices

The 1948 Act had no effect on cartels and other agreements restraining competition unless they were entered into by firms in a monopoly situation, when a monopoly reference could be made. Under the 1948 Act, the MRPC could be asked to investigate the general effect on the public interest of certain restrictive practices. In 1952, it was asked to report on the effect on the public interest of agreements and arrangements under which the participants were required to withhold supplies, to discriminate between purchases, or grant collective rebates. The Commission reported that these practices did operate against the public interest, but could not agree on the action to be taken. The majority wanted such practices, together with collective resale price maintenance, prohibited, while the minority preferred a system of registration and subsequent scrutiny. In the event the minority report was adopted and formed the basis of the Restrictive Trade Practices Act 1956. This Act, since amended, provided the framework of control for restrictive trading agreements. It established the office of the Registrar of Restrictive Trading Agreements (now taken over by the Director General of Fair Trading) and the Restrictive Practices Court.

The legislation, now contained in the Restrictive Trade Practices Act, 1976, deals with those agreements where at least two of the parties accept certain restrictions on their business activities, such as price fixing, market sharing, terms and conditions, and with whom to deal. Both goods and services are covered, as are information agreements relating to prices. The Act requires these agreements to be registered with the Office of Fair Trading, and unless the parties are prepared to modify an agreement to remove the offending restrictions, the Director must, with some exceptions, refer it to the Restrictive Practices Court.

The agreement is presumed to be contrary to the public interest unless the parties can satisfy the Court that the agreement satisfies one of the conditions laid down in the Act for validation, known as the 'gateways', and also that the agreement has benefits which outweigh any detriments. Thus, deliberate restrictions on competition are deemed to be, in general, not in the public interest, but the parties are given the opportunity to convince the Court otherwise by reference to specific criteria which are set out in the Act. Failure to register an agreement makes the agreement void, but it is not illegal to give effect to an unregistered agreement. Once an agreement is registered it has preliminary validity pending the decision of the Court.

Resale price maintenance, except for collective agreements of a horizontal nature, was excluded from the restrictive practices legislation, and it was not until 1964 that individual resale price maintenance was brought under control. Individual resale price maintenance is now covered by the Resale Prices Act, 1976, which makes any agreement as to minimum resale prices void, and it is unlawful for a manufacturer to refuse to supply his product because of the failure to observe a condition as to minimum resale prices by a dealer. It is open to a manufacturer to show to the Court that resale price maintenance in respect of his products is in the public interest. There have only been two successful cases, relating to books and certain pharmaceutical products.

The EEC Treaty also exercises control over restrictive trading agreements. Article 85 provides that all agreements which have the effect of restricting, preventing, or distorting competition within the Common Market, and which effect trade between Member States are prohibited and void, unless the EC Commission exempts them under the authority given to it. As with Article 86, certain conduct is thus prohibited and penalties can be applied for breaches of the rules, whereas the United Kingdom law only prohibits an agreement after it has been examined by the Court, and found to be contrary to the public interest.

Institutional background

Before examining in more detail the various areas of competition law, it would seem desirable to briefly describe the institutional background to the law. The main institutional bodies concerned with competition law and policy are:

(1) the Office of Fair Trading, and its main official, the Director General of Fair Trading;
(2) the Monopoly and Mergers Commission (MMC);
(3) the Restrictive Practices Court;
(4) the secretary of state; and
(5) the European Communities Commission and the European Court of Justice (ECJ).

The Office of Fair Trading

The Office of Fair Trading was established by the Fair Trading Act, 1973, and is the main body concerned with competition policy. Its chief official is the Director General of Fair Trading, and many statutory duties are placed on him. The main functions of the Director in relation to competition are:

(1) to keep under review commercial activity in the United Kingdom in order to be aware of practices which have an anti-competitive effect;
(2) to keep a register of restrictive trading agreements, and to bring all registered agreements, with certain exceptions, before the Restrictive Practices Court for a decision on whether the agreements are contrary to the public interest;
(3) to keep under review possible monopoly situations, and to make monopoly references to the MMC;
(4) to carry out a preliminary investigation to establish whether a particular course of conduct amounts to an anti-competitive practice, and, if appropriate, to make a competition reference to the MMC;
(5) to keep under review merger activity, and to make recommendations to the secretary of state as to whether or not a merger should be referred to the MMC; and

(6) to liaise with the EC Commission on Common Market competition matters.

One important feature is the independence from Government enjoyed by the Director in many areas. Thus he has the power himself to make monopoly and competition references. However, in some areas he can only give advice and recommendations to the secretary of state. This applies in merger and public body references, where only the secretary can make a reference to the MMC.

Monopoly and Mergers Commission

This was first created under another name by the 1948 Act, and its present role is defined by the Fair Trading Act, 1973. Its function is to investigate monopoly and merger situations, anti-competitive practices and the activities of public bodies which have been referred to it by either the Director or the secretary of state. The MMC cannot initiate references or take any action, though it can make recommendations for action.

The report is sent to the secretary of state, who may or may not act on its recommendations. The normal course is for the secretary of state to ask the Director to obtain voluntary undertakings from the firm or firms concerned. The Director is then under a duty to monitor the undertakings to see they are complied with.

Restrictive Practices Court

The Court was established by the Restrictive Trade Practices Act, 1956. Its role is to hear restrictive trading agreement and resale price maintenance cases referred to it by the Director, and decide whether they are, or are not, in the public interest. Unlike the reports of the MMC, the decisions of the Court are binding, both on the Director and the parties to the agreement.

The Secretary of State

Although many areas of competition policy have been taken out of the political arena, the secretary of state does have many important functions. His main roles in relation to competition are:

(1) to make monopoly references, a power he shares with the Director;
(2) to make merger and public body references;
(3) to authorize the Director not to make references to the Restrictive Practices Court where an agreement is of minor significance;
(4) to exempt from the restrictive practices legislation agreements of national importance; and
(5) to make orders following a report of the MMC.

EC Commission and the ECJ

The main task of seeing that Common Market competition law is complied with falls on the Commission. In dealing with breaches of the anti-trust laws, the Commission has the power to prohibit certain types of business behaviour, and can also impose fines and penalties on undertakings. The Commission does not only have a negative role, but can also promote a competitive structure. Thus, it has the power to exempt some agreements from the general prohibition contained in Article 85 where it feels that competition can be strengthened by such agreements. The Commission can also issue group or 'bloc' exemptions for certain categories of agreements.

The decisions of the Commission are subject to an appeal by companies or individuals to the ECJ, which is the final arbiter on questions of Common Market law. Its judgements are the ultimate authority on the anti-trust law of the EEC in respect of business activities. The ECJ also hears cases on competition law which have been referred to it by the courts of Member States under Article 177 of the Treaty, which provides that where a question of Community law is raised before the courts of a Member State, that court may, or if it is a final appeal court, shall, request the ECJ to give a ruling.

Conclusion

Competition or anti-trust law is almost entirely statutory, deriving either from United Kingdom or Common Market legislation. In the main it is enforced by administrative bodies rather than the courts, though the ECJ has an important role to play in connection with the anti-trust law of the EEC. This is probably inevitable, as it is an area of law which is closely related to economic policy, and therefore not particularly suitable for judicial reasoning.

An understanding of the law relating to competition and anti-trust is therefore difficult, if not impossible, without some appreciation of the economic theories and principles which lie behind the legal regulation. Legal analysis does not necessarily correspond with economic analysis, and the failure of economists to clearly identify workable competition makes it difficult to base anti-trust regulation on economic theory.

The next chapter will examine theories of competition and monopoly in an attempt to discover why anti-trust law is considered an essential feature of the economic policies of most western democracies. The remainder of the book will be concerned with examining the various forms of legal regulation, starting with monopoly and dominant positions and working through to restrictive agreements. A chapter will also be included on the effects of state involvement, through public ownership and state aids, on the competitive structure of the United Kingdom economy.

2

Economic Concepts of Competition

Introduction

The previous chapter has outlined the various channels through which the law can be brought to bear on issues concerning competition, and the following chapters examine these mechanisms in more detail. However, the rationale for competition policy is mainly economic and no indication has yet been given of the reasons why the law should become involved in economic activity in this way. This chapter, therefore, has four objectives:

(1) to show how mainstream economic analysis treats the ideas of competition and monopoly;
(2) to explain how this analysis provides a qualified rationale for government regulation of competitive conditions;
(3) to identify some of the limitations of the conventional theory, and to examine the implications of other approaches for the implementation of competition policy; and
(4) to examine various attempts to measure the cost of monopoly power.

It is important to appreciate from the beginning that the economic analysis is problematical and incomplete, and is currently undergoing potentially radical change. Different economists have different perspectives, and the same empirical facts may be interpreted in different ways, giving widely different policy recommendations on the same issues. Furthermore, none of the long-established competing theoretical frameworks are sufficiently operational to be applied at the level of detail required to formulate and guide practical policy in individual cases. Economists have not been able to produce a set of guidelines which clearly distinguish between those real-life situations which require intervention in the public interest and those where no intervention is required. Nor has economic analysis been able to identify the ideal form of intervention to be applied in situations where it is agreed that unregulated behaviour is unacceptable. To that extent, the economists have failed the policy-maker. On the other hand, economic analysis does provide a framework for analysis and a way of organizing our thinking about the very complex issues involved. Furthermore, some of the recent developments in the field offer the prospect of a much more operational analysis.

The remainder of this chapter is divided into a number of sections. The first two outline the standard economic analysis of competition and monopoly, which is to be found in the major textbooks, and whose findings provide the standard justifications for anti-trust policy. The next section examines some of the limitations of the simple approach, and the problems which have arisen when attempting to bring it to bear on more complex industrial situations. The fourth widens the debate to include some fundamental criticisms of the standard approach and the fifth examines the issues involved in attempting to measure the burden imposed by monopoly. Finally, before a brief concluding section, a short outline is provided of a recent development which may offer a way forward.

The optimal allocation of resources

At its simplest level, the rationale for policy towards competition is based on the argument that an economy performs better if the industries within it operate in a competitive way than if they do not. However, such a statement is not self-evident and can only be justified with reference to some clear idea of what is meant by 'better performance'. Such a framework is provided by the economic analysis outlined in this section.

Every economy, no matter how it is organized, has to produce the answer to three basic questions. These are:

(1) Which goods and services should be produced, and how much of each should be provided? While this can be put as a single question, it involves producing detailed answers to tens of millions of other questions, one for each commodity which the economy is capable of producing;

(2) How should each of these commodities be produced? Answering this question most obviously involves choosing the appropriate technique for each commodity (labour-intensive production or capital-intensive methods) but it also involves decisions on where to locate production and decisions on which individual workers should be involved in the production of which commodities; and

(3) Who gets what? How are the goods and services produced to be distributed between the different participants in the economic process.

There are essentially three ways in which these questions could be answered. First, they could be answered through 'custom' – society could have some pre-ordained set of rules which allowed the questions to be answered by reference to previous practice. Secondly, they could be answered by 'command', where those holding power simply decree their preferred answers to each question. Thirdly, they could be answered through a 'market mechanism'. It is this last method which dominates in unplanned economies, and whose workings are central to the whole debate on competition policy. It is therefore important to take a very brief look at the outlines of a market economy.

In a market economy the resource allocation decisions are not taken by any individual. Rather it is the case that the answers emerge from a decentralized decision-making process. The economy consists of millions of households and hundreds of thousands of firms. Households are concerned to distribute their available time, wealth and skills across a range of different activities in the ways which suit them best. Firms are mainly concerned to make profits. These two groups of economic factors are linked together through two sets of markets. First, there are the markets for goods and services. In these markets, firms supply those goods which are demanded by households who are willing to sacrifice part of their income and time in order to acquire them. Second, there are the markets for factors of production, including all the different types of resource which can be used to produce goods and services. In these markets, households are the suppliers, seeking to earn income, and firms are the demanders, seeking to buy or hire the resources they need in order to produce products. Out of this apparent chaos (some would say real chaos) come the detailed answers to the resource allocation questions outlined above. The fundamental question about such a social mechanism, and the one which underlies the whole range of issues concerning competition policy is simply 'How well does it work?'

Such a question can only be answered if there is some clear idea of what the system's objectives are and what constitutes 'good' performance. This is an obvious question, but an extremely difficult one to answer, without being too partial or specific or simply producing a long list of conflicting desiderata. Economists identify two basic objectives for any system of resource allocation. The first is that it should be 'efficient', the second is that it should be 'equitable'. Each of these objectives is important for competition policy and each requires elaboration.

'Efficiency' may be simply defined as getting maximum output from the resources available to the economy, and that definition is very similar to the definitions of efficiency used in engineering or physics. However, the economy's output consists of tens of millions of different items so that there is a problem in deciding what exactly is meant by 'maximum output'. In principle this can be resolved by noting that the real output of the economy is not goods and services, but rather the satisfaction which households and individuals derive from those goods and services. In that case 'economic efficiency' means organizing the economy in such a way that households derive maximum satisfaction from the combination of goods and services produced. At first sight such a definition may appear rather vague and theoretical. Nevertheless, it is possible to use it to identify the characteristics of an efficient allocation of resources at the level of an individual industry.

The diagrams in Figure 1 illustrate the major points. Figure 1(a) is a 'demand curve', showing the amounts which consumers are willing and able to buy at each price. If consumers are deemed to be rational and self-interested, then the price which a consumer is willing to pay for a unit of the commodity can conveniently be taken as a monetary

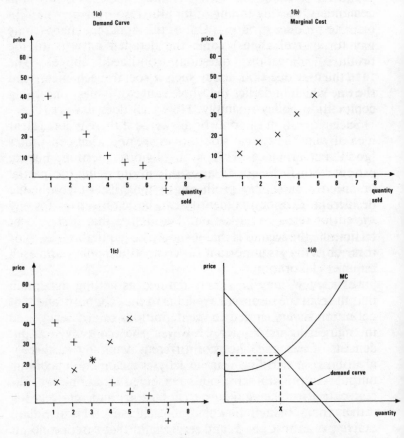

Figure 1   *The socially optimal quantity of a commodity.*

measure of the satisfaction he expects to get from having that unit of the commodity. In the figure shown, just one unit of the commodity will be sold if the price is £40, indicating that someone in the economy values that first unit at £40. Two units will be sold only if the price falls to £30, indicating that the second unit is valued at £30. The total value to consumers of two units of this product, then, is £70. Clearly, the total value of the commodity to the community increases as more units are produced, until we reach the point where so many units have been produced that no one is willing to pay for a further unit. If we considered a commodity which could be produced at zero cost, then, and we asked 'What is the economically efficient amount to produce?', then the answer would be six units. Somebody in the economy is willing to pay for (i.e. places a positive value on) the first six units produced, but no one is willing to pay for the seventh unit.

In the very simple example given, then, for the commodity shown, consumer satisfaction is maximized, and efficiency achieved, by producing six units of the commodity shown. However, most goods and services cannot be produced without cost, and it has to be remembered that each unit produced requires resources which could have been used to produce other things. Clearly, this needs to be taken into account when deciding on the most efficient level of output to produce. Figure 1(b) takes this point up. The points marked show the 'marginal cost' of producing each unit of the commodity, marginal cost being defined as the extra cost incurred in the production of each successive unit. As this cost effectively measures the value of the other things which could have been produced with the resources, then it should be clear that the efficient course of action is to produce each unit of a good for which the price consumers are willing to pay exceeds the marginal cost, but to go no further. In Figure 1(c), the demand curve and the cost curve are brought together, identifying the optimal output of this commodity as three units. As it is rather clumsy to present diagrams in a discontinuous fashion, Figure 1(d) shows the version which is usually to be found in the economic literature. This embodies exactly the same ideas, but assumes that the level of output can vary continuously, instead of jumping from one unit to two units without any intermediate position being possible. In the diagram given, the economically efficient level of output is X.

To sum up, then, economic efficiency will be achieved if an economy produces the amount of each commodity indicated by the intersection of the demand curve and the marginal cost curve for that commodity. In a market economy, of course, where commodities are sold, rather than distributed freely, the sale of the optimal level of output requires that the price be set equal to the marginal cost of producing the optimal quantity (P in Figure 1(d)). This requirement for price to equal marginal cost is important for the analysis of competition and monopoly, and also has applications in pricing for nationalized industries (see Webb, 1976 for a brief outline).

The second aim for any system of resource allocation is 'equity', or fairness. However, unlike efficiency, equity is not a concept on which economic analysis has very much to contribute. The economist has no definition of equity from which to derive optimal conditions, and the economic analysis of competition and monopoly is, therefore, almost entirely concerned with questions of efficiency. Clearly, this imposes limits on the ability of the economist to guide policy when equity is a major objective and this is particularly true of competition policy where many of the legal issues are framed in terms of the 'fairness' of prices or of agreements reached between companies and individuals. It is important to bear in mind that when an economist refers to 'a social optimum', or to the 'optimal allocation of resources', he is almost always referring to an efficient allocation of resources, without any further consideration of its equity.

Textbook models of competition and monopoly

Perfect competition and efficiency

The section above has shown what is meant by an efficient allocation of resources. This section is concerned to illustrate how the term 'competition' is interpreted in mainstream modern economics, and how it can be shown that a competitive economy will automatically achieve efficiency without any need for government intervention.

One of the most influential propositions ever put forward, which continues to have an enormous effect upon the conduct of economic affairs, is Adam Smith's suggestion that the forces of competition (the 'Invisible Hand') could lead to the reconciliation of private, self-interested behaviour with the general social good. Smith's analysis remains one of the richest contributions to social science, and the discussion of competition in his 1776 *Wealth of Nations* is full of insights which continue to be useful today. However, Smith's work contains no rigorous definition of competition and modern mainstream economics has tended to develop in a way which places a very high value on the clear specification of models, beginning with a set of assumptions and working through to the conclusions which follow from those assumptions. As a result of this process, the concept of competition has been progressively narrowed down until economists generally associate the term with a very particular type of industrial structure known as 'perfect competition'. A perfectly competitive industry is one which conforms to the following conditions:

(1) It contains a large number of small firms, selling to a large number of small customers. No producer or customer is sufficiently large to affect the market price of the commodity. In other words, if an individual producer withholds his output from the market, that will not push prices up, nor can an individual customer push prices down by refusing to purchase at the going price (It is worth noting from the outset that this condition effectively precludes any industry in which there are substantial economies of large scale production, because in such industries large firms have substantial cost advantages over smaller firms and such industries therefore tend to be highly concentrated.);

(2) All firms are aiming to make maximum profit;

(3) All firms produce exactly the same product, which is known to be identical by all customers;

(4) Entry to the industry is unrestricted, so that any entrepreneur who judges that he can make a profit in the industry can set up without hindrance, under exactly the same conditions as the established firms; and

(5)   Everyone concerned (customers, competitors, potential entrants) is perfectly informed of the market opportunities available.

If the conditions above hold, then it can be shown that economic efficiency, as defined above, will be automatically achieved. The details of the mechanisms involved need not detain us here (see Koutsoyannis, 1975 for a typical treatment), but a brief outline is useful.

Under the conditions specified, no firm has any market power. As far as each individual firm is concerned, the price of the industry's product is determined by market forces, and each firm has to accept that price and sell as much as will yield maximum profit. As the firm gets the same price for each unit of output it sells, regardless of the amount produced, the firm aiming for maximum profit will increase its output up to the level where the price it gets for a further unit sold is just equal to the extra cost incurred in producing that unit. In other words, price will be equal to marginal cost, giving the socially optimal result described above. This point is set out in more detail in Figure 2. Figure 2(a) shows the situation facing an individual firm in a perfectly competitive industry. The horizontal line *PD* shows the demand curve

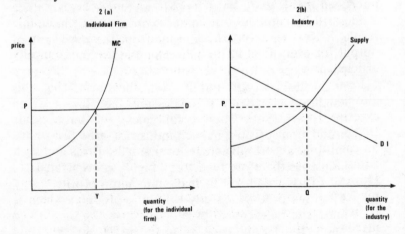

Figure 2   *The firm and industry in perfect competition.*

facing the firm, indicating that the firm can sell any amount at price P, but nothing at a higher price. The line MC shows the firm's marginal costs for each level of output. If the firm wishes to make maximum profit, it will choose to produce level of output Y. This situation facing each individual firm under 'atomistic competition' (another term sometimes used to describe perfect competition) is directly related to the overall industry position shown in Figure 2(b). This shows the demand curve for the product as a whole (as opposed to the demand for an individual firm's output shown in Figure 2 (a)) and the 'supply curve', which shows the amount of the product which firms in the industry will choose to produce at each price. The market price is determined by the intersection of these two curves, with price P and quantity Q. However, the supply curve is simply the marginal cost curve for the industry as a whole, showing as it does the amount which all firms taken together will choose to supply at each price (which is, of course, directly related to the marginal cost of each firm in the industry). A direct comparison of Figures 1(d) and 2(b) reveals that under perfect competition, the result which the market mechanism automatically produces is the same as the efficient result. This is a modern version of Smith's original 'Invisible Hand' proposition – that self-interested behaviour on the part of individuals, when moderated by competition, can provide a socially desirable result. Price will automatically equal the marginal cost of output for every firm in the industry, and the economically efficient level of output will be produced.

Perfect competition will also guarantee another result, although only in the long term. This is the elimination of any excess profits through the mechanism of perfectly free entry. If the established firms in the industry are making a return on capital which is larger than in other industries, then new firms will be attracted in, and they face no hindrance. However, their entry will tend to push down the price and render the industry less profitable until the return on capital is just equal to that which can be earned elsewhere. The mechanism of entry, or even simply the threat of entry, is an important aspect of the competitive process, not only in perfect competition, but also in more complex structures, and the conditions under which entry can take place are frequently of interest to those concerned with framing and implementing competition law.

The analysis above has illustrated the formal economic-analytical reasons for regarding perfect competition as an optimal form of market structure, which produces ideal results. However, in the broader context of competition policy and competition law, it is worth noting the very large gap between the model of perfect competition, and the everyday usage of the term. In common usage, the term 'competition' is generally taken to mean rivalry between protagonists, which is essentially an aspect of their behaviour. In the perfectly competitive model there is very little reference to the behaviour of firms, beyond the assumption that their aim is to maximize profits. 'Competition' is associated with the industry's structure (identical products, small firms, free entry), which is such that rivalry does not exist. Each firm faces 'the market', which sets the price, rather than identifiable rivals. Nothing an individual firm does will have a direct effect on any other individual firm. This conception of competition is, therefore, both limited and very different from the more vague, but richer and more complex notion of competition which underlies much of the law.

Monopoly and misallocation

The model of 'perfect competition' is matched by an equally rigorous model of 'pure' monopoly, defined as an industry in which there is only one firm, and there is no possibility of future entry. In that case, it can be shown quite simply that the industry's performance will be sub-optimal.

Figure 3 shows the demand curve and the marginal cost curve which featured in Figures 1 and 2, with the optimal levels of output and price given by Q and P. If the industry is in the hands of a single firm then these are the curves for that firm, as well as for the industry as a whole. However, such a firm is in a more powerful position than the individual perfect competitor because the price it can charge will depend upon the level of output it chooses to produce and sell. By restricting output to X, for instance, it can raise price to Y. In this situation, the firm will not make maximum profit by

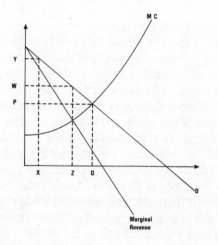

Figure 3 *Price and output under monopoly.*

choosing the level of output where price equals marginal cost (output *Q*), but rather by producing less, limiting output to the level where marginal cost equals the increase in revenue earned by producing one more unit (marginal revenue). This is shown in Figure 3 as output level *Z*, which will be sold at price *W*. However, if this level of output is produced, economic efficiency will be lost. There are a number of units of output, between *Z* and *Q*, which consumers value more highly than the cost of the resources required to produce them. In the interests of efficiency, then, they should be produced and failure to do so means a loss of social welfare.

The first charge levelled at monopoly, then, is that it leads to economic inefficiency. Price will be higher than marginal cost, and output will be lower than is socially optimal. The second charge is slightly different, but corresponds more closely to common-sense complaints about monopoly behaviour. This is the charge that a firm in a monopoly position will have the freedom to allow its costs to rise above the minimum level necessary, without suffering any penalty. Economists are obliged to give this aspect of inefficiency a new name, having (confusingly) requisitioned the word 'efficiency' to mean 'economic efficiency' or 'price equal to marginal cost'. Such behaviour is most frequently described as 'managerial inefficiency' or 'X-inefficiency'.

It is important to note that if a firm is X-inefficient then it is not making the maximum profit available to it, and this will only be possible if the managers of the company actually have the discretion to be slack in this way. Obviously, in a monopoly situation, managers are not under any pressure from the competition (that is the very basis of the X-inefficiency charge against monopoly). However, there are other sources of pressure on them. Shareholders may monitor the returns they receive, especially if they are large organizations like pension funds, insurance companies or other financial institutions who employ professional managers for that purpose. A management team which fails to make full use of its opportunities for profit may be ousted. It is also worth noting that directors of a company, who have the ability to control managers directly, are usually also shareholders.

Pressure to maintain maximum profits may also come via the 'market for corporate control', i.e. the market for voting shares in a company. If a firm is making less profit than it could, then its share price will be lower than it could be, and this will make the company attractive to 'take-over' raiders who may attempt to buy the relatively under-valued shares, turn the company around (often at the expense of the jobs or status of the existing management) and see a capital gain when the company's improved performance is reflected in higher share prices. This mechanism may work through take-overs actually taking place, but that is not necessary. The threat that take-over may follow from sub-optimal performance may be enough (see Holl, 1977).

Another form of pressure on companies to make maximum profit is to be found in the managerial labour markets which are internal to companies. Fama (1980) has suggested that an individual manager may face pressure from both above and below to perform in ways which lead the company to aim for maximum profit, even when managers are not themselves shareholders.

Beyond 'perfect' competition and 'pure' monopoly

Limitations of the simple models

The most common criticism of the models of 'perfect' competition and 'pure' monopoly is that they are unrealistic, as markets which conform to their very tight specifications are rare or perhaps even non-existent. However, for some of the purposes for which economic analysis is intended, lack of realism is not necessarily a valid criticism. If the aim of an economic theory is to cut through the complications of real life, in order to give a manageable model whose fundamental purpose is to predict how parts of the economy may behave, then unrealistic assumptions may have an important part to play.

If we were concerned to use economic models solely for predictive purposes then the unrealism of perfect competition and pure monopoly need not concern us too much. However, if the analysis is to be used for 'normative' purposes, that is to make statements about how the economy should behave, and what sort of policy should be introduced, then the problems are real. If we wish to use economic analysis to decide whether one real-world situation is superior to another, and neither conforms closely to either 'pure' model, then it is difficult to see how the polar models can be used to discriminate effectively.

One method which might be used to bring the models to bear on policy would be to argue that most industries are a fair approximation to either perfect competition or monopoly. Those which are virtually monopolies should be regulated, in order to force them to behave competitively, while those which conform roughly to competitive conditions can reasonably be left alone. Unfortunately, this argument suffers from at least two flaws. In the first place, it can be very difficult to measure just how closely an industry approximates to either pure competition or monopoly and to draw the dividing line between those which are 'approximately competitive' and those which are 'approximate monopolies'. A perfectly competitive industry has one characteristic which concerns the behaviour of firms (they all attempt to maximize profits), one which concerns the state of information (everyone concerned has perfect knowledge of market opportunities) and three characteristics which concern the structure of the industry (large number of small firms, free entry, identical products). 'Closeness' to perfect competition then is a question of how closely five qualitatively different conditions are met in a particular industry, a distinctly elusive concept.

Secondly, and even more fundamentally, there is the issue known to economists as the 'second-best' problem. It has been shown above that perfect competition will give an optimal allocation of resources in an individual industry. If every industry is perfectly competitive then the economy as a whole will achieve the maximum satisfaction of households, given the limited resources available. That result is known as the 'first-best' optimum. However, in the real economy there are some industries which cannot possibly be perfectly competitive, and which cannot be forced to meet the required condition that price equals marginal cost. In that case, the 'first-best' optimum is completely unattainable, and the question becomes 'What is the second-best optimum?', i.e. the best position actually achievable?

This is a question to which economic analysis provides a rather depressing answer because it is simply not possible to identify the detailed characteristics of the second-best position, which will inevitably vary, depending upon the particular distortion (more likely many distortions) which cannot be removed. As if this were not bad enough, what analysis does show is that if one of the conditions for the 'first-best' optimum is not achieved, then the others may no longer be desirable and indeed may be counter-productive. Consider the simple example, for instance, of an economy where every market and industry is perfectly competitive except for the coal industry, which is a private sector monopoly which cannot be controlled. In that case, coal will be priced above marginal cost and too little coal will be produced, relative to the optimum level. However, because markets throughout the economy are inter-connected, this will have a number of other effects. In the perfectly competitive gas industry, demand will be higher than it would be in a perfect economy, because consumers will turn from high-priced coal to gas, and as a result 'too much' gas will be produced. For this distortion to be offset, it might actually be better for the gas industry to also be a monopoly, in order to lean against the distorting effect of the coal monopoly. This is only one part of the problem, of course, because in every industry which uses coal as an input costs will cease to be a reflection of the true value of the resources used, being also a reflection of the monopoly power of the coal producer. In an economy which is perfectly competitive everywhere, the marginal cost of everything is an equal to its price, which is a measure of the value placed upon it by consumers. Once a distortion is introduced, then this ceases to be true, and the argument that an individual perfectly competitive industry produces the optimal level of output ceases to be true because demand and costs will partly reflect the 'wrong' prices which hold in other parts of the economy.

Clearly, the problem of second-best is very destructive of the attempt to identify in detail the optimal conditions under which an economy should operate and it is tempting, as Webb (1976) puts it, 'to throw up one's hands' and give up the attempt. However, it is possible to salvage something from the wreckage by noting that not all interrelationships in the economy are of equal significance. If an industry operates in relative isolation from others which are functioning imperfectly then it may be quite legitimate to treat it on a piecemeal basis, applying the general rules set out above.

The search for 'workable competition'

If perfect competition is not achievable in many sectors of industry, then one possible response is to attempt to identify 'workable competition', defined by Clarke (1940) as:

> the most desirable forms of competition, selected from those that are practically possible, within the limits set by conditions which we cannot escape.

Unfortunately, however, we have very little to guide us in deciding what would constitute such desirable forms, and the second-best problem outlined above makes it clear that approximating to perfect competition is not the answer. Clarke certainly recognized this, and provided one of the earliest statements of the second-best problem. However, as Lee (1979) notes, its implications have not been given sufficient emphasis by successive writers in their attempts to further define 'workable competition', and as a result most such attempts are tautological (defining workable competition as that which gives the best available result), unworkably vague, or demonstrably incorrect. Attempts to identify workability usually consist of long lists of structural and behavioural 'norms' which an industry should achieve before being deemed workably competitive. As many of the norms amount to approximations to perfect competition, it is difficult to see how the application of such listings could be of advantage, or what has been gained through the search for 'workability'. One observer (Stigler, 1956) has rather cynically noted that it is simple to decide whether an industry is workably competitive or not. All that is required is that an able graduate student write a dissertation on the subject. There is, however, a further condition, which is that no other student should ever be allowed to decide whether the same industry conforms or not, as he would be bound to reach the opposite conclusion!

Although economic analysis has failed to find satisfactory criteria for 'workable' competition, it is worth noting that the law on competition often seems to implicitly assume that some (undefined) version does exist and is understood. Hay and Morris (1979) suggest that the *'per se'* approach of US anti-trust, in particular, implies a presumption that at least some characteristics of a workably competitive market are known. Indeed, it could be argued that any non-discretionary approach to monopoly policy, which outlaws certain market structures, or certain practices, involves the assumption that such practices are known to be inconsistent with workable competition, which in turn implies that the concept has been identified. Obviously, if such an assumption does lie behind competition laws, then they are only weakly based in economic analysis.

Structure, conduct and performance

The search for 'workable competition' has been one response to the inadequacies of standard theory for the design of policy. Another has been to turn away from theory and to attempt to examine the facts of industries' operation in order to identify those factors which lead companies to behave in unacceptable ways, and those which lead to satisfactory performance. This route was suggested as the way forward by Mason, as long ago as 1937, when he notes that:

> It is not . . . sufficient to conduct purely analytical and descriptive studies of various types of control situation . . . A further study of different types of industrial markets and business practices and of the effects on prices, outputs, investment and employment designed to indicate means of distinguishing between socially desirable and undesirable situations . . . is the only way in which economics can contribute directly to the shaping of public policy.

This challenge has been taken up in America and to a lesser extent in the UK, with groups of economists using increasingly sophisticated statistical methods to attempt to identify the empirical links between industries' performance, their structure and the conduct of the companies within them. The relationships examined vary in their details, but in general they hypothesize that profitability (or price/cost margins) will be positively related to the level of seller concentration (i.e. the extent to which the industry is in the hands of a small number of firms), to the height of entry-barriers (i.e. the difficulties faced by potential entrants), to the extent of product differentiation through advertising, and to the rate of growth of demand. Some of the studies also include the proposition that profits or margins will be negatively related to competition from imports.

As with so many issues, opinions vary on the value of the structure–conduct–performance approach to industry behaviour. On the positive side of the argument, it could be noted that many (though by no means all) of the studies have confirmed the existence of a positive relationship between the level of concentration and the level of profits, thereby suggesting to some writers, that concentration confers monopoly power which in turn allows higher profits to be earned and which therefore justifies government regulation of highly concentrated industries. However, there are a number of reasons why such a conclusion cannot be held with any great confidence.

In the first place, there are problems of statistical method, which make it difficult to measure the various different concepts used and to unravel the extent of the links between them. Most of the central concepts − concentration, entry barriers, product differentiation − are difficult to measure and have to be approximated rather unsatisfactorily through the use of 'proxies'. As a result, the findings have tended to be very sensitive to the samples chosen and the sources of data, so that very similar studies produce contrasting, even diametrically opposite, results.

Secondly, there are problems with the mis-specification of the relationships between the variables. In the simple standard approach to structure–performance investigations, it is usually taken for granted that the direction of causation runs from industry structure to industry performance. However, even within the confines of a simple model like that of perfect competition it is clear that performance (a high level of profits for instance) can have an impact on structure (by inducing more firms to enter). If the relationships between structure and performance work in both directions then the results of simple statistical techniques tell us very little about the industry's workings, and a more complex model is required (see Phillips, 1976).

The third problem is even more fundamental, because it concerns the interpretation of the results, and the use to which they are put. If we accept, for the sake of argument, that the evidence shows a factual link between profitability and high levels of concentration, the most common interpretation placed on that fact is that a high level of concentration bestows monopoly power on firms, which in turn allows them to make monopoly profits, which reflect a misallocation of resources. The conclusion to be drawn for policy, then, is that concentration is a 'bad thing' and that there are gains to be had from an active policy against concentration and mergers. However, as Demsetz (1973, 1974) and others have noted, the same factual relationship between concentration and profitability could arise from a wholly different mechanism. It is perfectly possible that higher profits are simply the result of greater efficiency and that high levels of concentration are simply the incidental result of output becoming concentrated in the hands of those companies who have 'got it right'. If the cost structure for an industry exhibits substantial economies of scale, or if a few firms have management teams which happen to 'click' when others don't, then the industry may become concentrated in a few highly profitable firms, with results which have very little to do with the pure monopolist's raising of price through the restriction of output.

There are, therefore, two completely different lines of thought about the implications of the concentration–profitability relationship. The 'market power' interpretation sees it as evidence of powerful companies' ability to acquire and use costly monopoly power. The 'competitive' view argues that concentration may be the result of a desirable competitive process. Attempts have been made to devise tests which would allow us to decide between these conflicting hypotheses (see Clarke et al., 1984) but they are inconclusive, and it is very unlikely that any definitive conclusion will ever be reached to everyone's satisfaction.

Unfortunately, then, while the response to Mason's challenge has led to an improvement in our understanding of the issues involved, and very considerable refinement of both theoretical and statistical methods, it has not fulfilled the aspirations of those who hoped that an appeal to the facts over the head of theory would help in the construction of policy.

Competition as a process, rather than a state

The 'competitive' interpretation of the concentration–profitability relationship clearly implies a very different conception of competition from that derived from the perfectly competitive model, and it is important to appreciate the alternative notions of competition which co-exist in economic analysis.

In most of the early economists' work on competition (see McNulty, 1967), including that of Adam Smith, the picture of competition which is put forward is essentially one of rivalry between companies, a conception of competition which is not far from the everyday use of the term. However, as noted above, the precise conditions for such competition were not spelt out and the predilection of modern economists for tightly specified models with conclusions following rigorously from an explicit set of assumptions has meant that the notion of 'perfect competition' has tended to supersede the earlier notions of competition, at least in the textbooks. This narrow conception of competition is very different from the everyday use of the term and has a number of characteristics which limit its usefulness.

First, the perfectly competitive model is completely static and contains no reference to behaviour over time. The basic picture of the economy which it represents is one of a group of households who have fixed tastes with respect to a set of known products, facing a group of firms having an unchanging set of technologies available to them. Everybody is perfectly informed about everything and the abstract forces of supply and demand ensure that consumer satisfaction is maximized. Emphasis is placed on how an industry will behave in equilibrium. In that type of model, profits are only a temporary aberration, which are eliminated in the long-run. If the demand for a product should happen to increase, then firms in that industry will earn high profits, that will attract new entrants, and then the industry will settle to a new equilibrium, again with no excess profits being earned. Such a model has no room for the entrepreneur, for unthought-of innovations, or for rivalry between individual firms.

An alternative view of competition, which links back to the earlier notions, is that which has become known as the 'Austrian' view (see Reekie, 1979 for a brief introduction). In this view, competition is not a state, as in 'perfect competition', but rather a process taking place through time in a world which is never in equilibrium, where all the possibilities are not known to everyone, where firms have differing abilities and where the entrepreneur who exercises creativity and foresight is able to alter the world he inhabits in ways which allow him to make profits. In this view of the world, profits may still be made as a result of a company having a monopoly position. However, unless the monopoly arises from some government-imposed restriction on competition or the sole ownership of a resource which has no substitute, it will tend to be a temporary one as other firms recognize the opportunities and enter the industry, or devise substitute products for the one which is earning high prices and profits. Indeed, in the Austrian view, some entrepreneurs are constantly trying to become temporary monopolists by being the first to invent a new product, or identify a new market, while others are constantly trying to break down existing temporary monopolies by entering markets which are seen to offer the prospect of profits.

Clearly, then, the Austrian view has quite radical implications for the interpretation of profits made, and for policy towards competition. If the notion of competition as a dynamic process is superior to the static conception purveyed in the economics textbooks, then the existence of profits is at least partly the result of socially beneficial creative behaviour, the disadvantages of monopoly have been over-stated, and it would be a mistake to introduce policies designed to eliminate excess profits. To that extent the Austrian view can be used to guide policy. What is much more difficult, once the benchmark of perfect competition is abandoned, is to decide what detailed form a policy should take. Littlechild (1981) suggests that case-studies of individual firms might allow some separation of the different sources of profits, presumably with action being taken in those cases where monopoly rents, as opposed to windfall or entrepreneurial profits, prevail. Demsetz (1969) has suggested that it might be possible to adopt a 'comparative institutions' approach, comparing the likely development of the market process under different types of policy regime. However, it is difficult to see how this would be achieved in detail. Perhaps the only clear prescription, which is held in common with the more orthodox approach to competition, is to see the removal of entry-barriers as a major focus for competition policy.

Measuring the cost of monopoly power

The introductory analysis described above has shown that if there is monopoly power, in the sense that prices are set above marginal cost, then the allocation of resources will be less than perfect, and there will be a corresponding 'efficiency loss'. However, that in itself says nothing about the size of the loss involved. When it is considered that the establishment and implementation of an anti-monopoly policy in itself involves the use of scarce and expensive resources, then it is important to consider whether the losses caused by monopoly are sufficiently large to justify the expenditure involved in attempting to correct it. Various writers have attempted to estimate the social costs of monopoly power, with radically different results depending upon the method of calculation and, more importantly, upon different interpretations of the nature of competition and the source of profits.

The mechanics of the measurement process are too complex to detail here, but in essence they begin from the proposition that monopoly power will reduce consumer satisfaction, as prices are raised above marginal cost, and increase profits. Published figures for profits are then used as a means of identifying the size of the loss involved.

The earliest attempt to measure the cost of monopoly power in this way was carried out by Harberger (1954), who concluded that the loss was in fact very slight, at about 0.1 per cent of national income (for the United States), a figure which has been refined but not radically altered by others who also found losses due to monopoly to be small.

Clearly, if such estimates are correct, then it is questionable whether a policy designed to reduce monopoly power is worthwhile at all. However, as might be expected, other analysts have criticized the basic method and produced very much larger estimates. Some of the criticisms are relatively technical, concerning the detail of the methods used to make the calculations, but others are of general interest. One such is the suggestion that the losses associated with sub-optimal prices and outputs are only part of the social loss caused by monopoly. It should also be noted that monopolists use up scarce resources in attempting to secure a monopoly position, and the cost of those resources should be added in to the losses attributable to monopoly. To follow the reasoning adopted by Posner (1975), if acquiring a monopoly position is itself a competitive activity, the cost of becoming a monopolist will just equal the monopoly profits to be made from acquiring the monopoly position. In that case the cost of monopoly is much higher than the estimates arrived at by Harberger and other writers using similar methods. Cowling and Mueller (1978) extended these arguments to calculate a number of different estimates of the loss due to monopoly using data for individual companies, rather than whole industries. They concluded that for the United States the losses attributable to a single firm (General Motors) amounted to $1.75 billion, which exceeded Herberger's estimate for the whole economy, and that the overall losses associated with the 734 largest firms could be as high as 13 per cent of the gross output of those firms. For the British case, it was concluded that monopoly losses could be as high as 7 per cent of output, with three firms alone (BP, Shell and BAT) accounting for losses of £186 million.

Clearly, if these latter estimates are correct, then the losses arising from monopoly power are very considerable, and the case for anti-monopoly policy is strengthened. Furthermore, the estimates of the losses attributable to individual firms could provide what Cowling and Mueller describe as 'the logical starting point for intensified enforcement of anti-trust policy'. However, this takes the debate back to the issue raised above, concerning the 'market power' versus the 'competitive' approach to concentration and to profits. Littlechild (1981), in particular, has argued that the whole conceptual framework used by Cowling and Mueller introduced an upward bias into the calculation of monopoly losses, which are therefore considerably exaggerated. The basic problem is that all the attempts to measure the cost of monopoly power take place within a framework of long-run equilibrium. The investigators assume that the profits which they observe, and which are used to calculate the welfare losses, are profits which can be maintained in the long-run and which are entirely due to the monopoly position held by the firms. Under that assumption, all profits represent welfare losses. However, that is a very strong assumption and if the industries being observed are not in long-run equilibrium at the moment of observation then the profits and price/cost margins observed cannot be attributed to monopoly power. For instance, even in a perfectly competitive industry, large profits may be made in the short-run, if the demand for the product suddenly increases. This cannot continue for long, because the profits will attract new entrants whose competition will eventually push the price back down to the level of average cost. Nevertheless, high levels of profit may be maintained for some time, even in the total absence of monopoly power, and in the total absence of welfare losses due to monopoly.

Observed returns to companies, then, can be divided into three components. First, there are true monopoly profits, which arise from a firm being completely protected in some way from competition, either through some form of government action (the grant of a patent, for instance) or through some permanent advantage held (perhaps sole ownership of some input for which there are no substitutes, or very powerful customer preference).

Second, there are temporary 'windfall' profits, which arise as a matter of luck, because cost or demand conditions turned out to be more favourable than anyone expected, so that even companies in competitive industries enjoy a period of high profit, until potential competitors see the opportunity and move in. (It should be noted that 'windfall' losses will also be made by firms and in industries where cost and demand conditions turn out to be less favourable than expected.)

Thirdly, echoing the Austrian view of competition, there will be an element of 'entrepreneurial' profit. Some firms have a greater ability than others to identify profitable opportunities, or to go further and to actually create opportunities which did not exist before. The profits resulting from this superior entrepreneurial ability do not arise from their having monopoly power, because the opportunities are in principle open to any firm.

The fundamental criticism, then, which can be levelled at most attempts to measure the cost of monopoly power, is that the investigators have assumed that all profits are the direct result of monopoly power, when it could be argued that some of the profits made are simply the result of unforeseen circumstances, and some are the result of being the first to spot or to create a new opportunity which henceforth becomes open to all.

'Contestable markets': a new approach to industry structure

The sections above have described the mainstream economic analysis of monopoly and competition and contrasted it with the rather different approach of the 'Austrian' theorists. It remains for this section to provide a very brief introduction to a recent development which has been described as a revolution in monopoly theory and which may offer a prospect of resolving some of the difficulties. In some respects the new approach has elements in common with the Austrian view, in that its general conclusions are that an industry may perform in a socially acceptable way even if it contains a very small number of firms, and does not therefore correspond even remotely to the specification of perfect competition. However, the genesis of the new approach lies very much in the mainstream of industrial economic theory, and it has the advantage of resting upon conventional analytical foundations.

> The new approach to industry structure is known as the theory of 'contestable markets'. The major aim of the theorists has been to provide the building blocks of a new theory of industrial organization . . . which . . . will transform the field and render it far more applicable to the real world. (Bailey, 1982)

As might be expected for a work with such ambitious objectives, the theory of contestable markets involves a number of new concepts, and a level of technical difficulty which puts a detailed treatment far beyond the scope of this chapter. Moreover, the analysis is not solely or even mainly directed towards questions of competition policy, and its implications in that direction have not been fully explored. Nevertheless, the findings are of sufficient importance to warrant a brief outline.

The major new concept which requires explanation is that of 'contestability'. A perfectly contestable market is one in which entry is free, exit is costless, existing firms and entrants compete on equal terms and potential entrants are not deterred from entering by the threat of retaliatory price-cutting by incumbents. In such a market it can be shown that the benefits previously associated with perfect competition alone will accrue, even if there are very few firms in the industry. As the contestability theorists themselves put it:

> Monopolists and oligopolists who populate such markets are sheep in wolves' clothing, for under this arrangement potential rivals can be as effective as actual competitors in forcing pro-social behaviour upon incumbents, whether or not such behaviour is attractive to them. As we have seen . . . this may be true where observed market phenomena are far from the competitive norm, and even where they superficially assume some pattern of behaviour previously thought to be pernicious *per se*. (Baumol, Panzar and Willig, 1982, p. 350)

Obviously, the idea of a contestable market is related to the idea of entry-barriers and such a market might be thought of as one where barriers to entry are relatively limited. However, the new theory also suggests that in many instances entry barriers are less formidable than has often been assumed. In particular, the analysis points to the importance of sunk costs as the major real deterrent to entry. (Sunk costs, as the name implies, are those costs which cannot be eliminated, even by cessation of production.) If sunk costs are small, then new entrants may have little difficulty in competing with existing firms on equal terms and the threat of this competition will force incumbents to behave like perfect competitors.

A good example, provided by Baumol *et al.* (1982), is a small airline market. If we consider the market for air travel between two small towns, where the number of people travelling is only sufficient to fill one aircraft per day, we have an example of a 'natural monopoly'. It will always be cheaper for the route to be serviced by a single airline than for two planes to fly in competition, and we would expect that market to be monopolized, in the sense of there being only one supplier. However, that one supplier will not be free to behave like a textbook monopolist. If aircraft can be rented, or if there is an active second-hand market for planes, then sunk costs are very limited. All an entrant need do, if the incumbent 'monopolist' is creating a profitable opportunity by charging high fares, is to fly his aircraft on to the tarmac, undercut the incumbent and make a profit. If the incumbent then cuts his price, the entrant can literally fly away, and either use the plane on another route or sell it (or cease renting it). The absence of substantial sunk costs make entry cheaply reversible and the threat or the reality of easy entry will discipline the incumbent 'monopolist'. Air travel, then, provides a useful example of a contestable market and its outcome.

The contestable markets approach has a number of implications for policy towards competition. First, it shows quite clearly that it is not appropriate to decide on whether to intervene in an industry by making reference to the degree of departure from the conditions of perfect competition. That in itself is not particularly new, as has been noted above. However, what is new is that the theory provides an alternative benchmark to the unattainable criterion of perfect competition, that of contestability, and suggests that policies designed to improve contestability are the most appropriate form of competition policy. When considering the structure and behaviour of an individual industry, the first step is to decide whether or not it constitutes a contestable market. If it does, then government interference is not needed, even if the industry exhibits symptoms which in the past have been accepted as indicators of poor market performance, such as high concentration, price discrimination, mergers and horizontal or vertical integration. If, on the other hand, the industry is not contestable then intervention in order to make it so needs to be considered. Most obviously, governments need to consider methods by which entry and exit to an industry can be made easier. In particular, policies are needed which reduce sunk costs, the main impediment to contestability. Such measures could include having sunk costs borne by government, which would then lease facilities to firms, or by mandating that sunk costs be shared by a consortium. Alternatively, sunk costs might be reduced by tax advantages for rapid depreciation, for re-tooling, or for the re-use of old plant in new activities. Anything which improves the market for second-hand capital equipment will also be useful.

Clearly, the contestable markets approach to competition involves a radical departure from the earlier approaches derived from the idea of perfect competition, the structure–conduct–performance model, or the notion of workable competition. It also has radical implications for the form of competition policy and competition law. However, as it is a relatively recent development, there has been insufficient time for it to have had any substantial influence on the legislation. The economic rationale for the law outlined in the following chapters has more in common with the traditional views than with the theory of contestable markets.

Summary and Conclusions

Economists are renowned for their failure to agree, and the analysis of competition and competition policy provides no exception. Nevertheless, this overview does provide a background to the more detailed consideration of the law which follows in later chapters.

Perhaps the most important point to note in conclusion is that the concept of competition has a number of different dimensions. The first concerns the structure of an industry, with the number of firms and the conditions of entry being of central importance. Secondly, there is the dimension of company behaviour, encompassing the basic aims of firms and the methods they adopt to achieve those aims (which may include attempts to secure and exploit a monopoly position). Thirdly, there is the dimension of industry performance, particularly with respect to prices charged, profits earned, levels of cost and, more fundamentally, efficiency and equity. The law is concerned with both structure and behaviour because of their perceived impact on performance, as the following chapters reveal.

The second point to be made, referring back to the introduction to this chapter, is that economic analysis has not provided the law-maker with a clear set of guidelines concerning the types of structure and behaviour which lead to acceptable performance. Despite the fact that the rationale for competition law is basically economic, the connection between the law and the economics is much more limited than might be expected, or hoped for.

3

Monopoly control

Introduction

It has been shown in the previous chapter that a company holding a monopoly position may be able to inflict social damage. However, that in itself is not enough to automatically condemn high levels of industrial concentration. In many cases such concentration arises as the result of scale economies. If the cost structure of an industry is such that the larger the scale of the operation, the lower the costs, then competition will paradoxically tend to lead to output becoming concentrated in the hands of a few firms, as larger firms out-compete smaller rivals. Clearly, such concentration is desirable in so far as it allows commodities to be produced at low cost, and for that reason governments often actively promote the process of concentration.

Even if scale economies are not important in an industry, and high levels of concentration have arisen in other ways, there is no certainty that dominant firms will make unacceptable use of their market power. Nevertheless, the potential for inefficient or inequitable behaviour remains and governments normally seek some kind of control over such industries.

This chapter is concerned with the English law on the control of monopoly. The most general point to be made by way of introduction is that, unlike United States law, the English law does not condemn what it defines as a monopoly *per se*. It does provide powers that enable a monopoly situation to be investigated in order to see if it is operating against the public interest. It is the abuse of monopoly power that is condemned, not monopoly power as such.

Powers and duties of the Director General of Fair Trading

The Director has a duty, under section 2 of the Fair Trading Act, 1973, to keep monopoly situations under review. This is done in two ways. In the first place the Director monitors the economic performance of industries in order that particular sectors can be identified for more detailed analysis. Published data is collected on aspects of market structure, and these are examined to see if there is evidence of high degrees of concentration. Particular stress is given to pricing, profits and market behaviour.

Secondly, the Director receives complaints by firms and consumers about various trading practices which they believe to be unfair. Many of these complaints may relate to the existence of a monopoly situation, and enquiries following these complaints may lead him to exercise his statutory powers to make a monopoly reference to the Monopolies and Mergers Commission (MMC).

However, it should be pointed out that even though the Director believes that a monopoly situation exists, he is not bound to make a reference, as this power is discretionary. The receipt of a complaint, or a request for a reference to be made, does not put the Director under any obligation. Neither is he limited in the making of a reference to matters which have been the subject of a complaint.

Seeking information

By the monitoring process and receiving complaints the Director may suspect that a monopoly situation exists, but requires further information about market share before deciding whether or not to make a reference. The power to seek information is given by sections 44 and 45 of the Fair Trading Act, 1973.

Under section 44, the Director has the power to require any person by, or to whom, the goods or services in question are supplied to supply him with information regarding the value, cost, price, or quantity or extent of the goods or services in question, together with the capacity of the undertaking and the numbers employed in relation to the specified goods or services.

With complex monopoly situations, that is those which involve investigating behaviour as well as structure, the Director needs not only information about market share, but also information as to agreements, arrangements and concerted practices which may restrict competition. Section 45 gives the Director the power, subject to the approval of the secretary of state, to require specified persons who may be so conducting their affairs so as to restrict competition between them to provide him with information about these practices, in circumstances where he has reason to believe that a complex monopoly situation exists. Wilful failure to provide information, or to give false information is an offence. The Director's powers are limited to seeking information for the sole purpose of deciding whether to make a reference.

Monopoly situation

Definition

Monopoly situations are defined in sections 6, 7 and 8 of the Act. In relation to goods, it exists where at least one-quarter of goods of a particular description are supplied in the United Kingdom by or to one person, a group of associated corporate bodies, or two of more persons who so conduct their affairs so as to restrict competition between them. A monopoly situation also exists where, because of agreements or arrangements, goods of a certain description are not supplied in the United Kingdom at all (section 6). Section 7 provides a similar definition in relation to services.

The test of a monopoly situation is that of supply and not production or consumption, and the goods or services in relation to sections 6 and 7 must be supplied in the United Kingdom. If, for example, firm A produced 70 per cent of a particular product and firm B 30 per cent, and A exported 90 per cent of its output, while B sold the whole of its output to the United Kingdom market, then A would not be in a monopoly situation in relation to that market, while B would. A similar result would be obtained if A was a subsidiary of another company, and supplied 90 per cent of its output to its parent company, as for the purpose of monopoly legislation, a group of associated companies are treated as one person.

Section 8 covers monopoly situations in relation to exports. A monopoly situation in relation to exports is taken to exist where at least one quarter of the goods of the description exported are produced in the United Kingdom by one person, or a group of associated corporate bodies, both in relation to exports generally, or in relation to a particular market. A monopoly situation also exists if agreements or arrangements are in operation which prevent, restrict or distort competition in relation to the export of goods generally, or to a particular market.

The definition of a monopoly situation in relation to exports refers to the production of goods, and not to the share of exports. The reasoning here is that to look at shares of exports would be to ignore a decision by a dominant firm not to export at all. But, as Cunningham (1974) points out, this does not necessarily follow. A firm may produce more than 25 per cent of United Kingdom production but consume all its own production and export nothing in that form. Alternatively, it may supply the home market with one type of quality, leaving the export market to be supplied by a number of other producers with other types or quality. An agreement or arrangement between a number of firms, who together form more than 25 per cent of the relevant market, not to export would be caught by the provisions relating to a behavioural or complex monopoly.

Structural and complex monopoly

It has been seen that a monopoly situation can be defined by reference to structural or behavioural factors. A structural monopoly is one where a single firm, or a group of associated firms, have at least 25 per cent of the relevant market. There is no need to investigate behaviour in a structural situation to discover whether a monopoly exists, the mere fact of market share being sufficient, though of course an investigation into behaviour will be necessary to discover if anything is being done to exploit a monopoly situation.

An investigation of market share is insufficient in relation to behavioural monopolies, or complex monopolies as they are referred to by the Act. As well as examining the market, it is also in this situation necessary to look at the behaviour of firms within the market, as the Act refers to persons who so conduct their affairs so as to restrict, prevent or distort competition between them.

The difference between a structural and a complex or behavioural monopoly situation can be illustrated by the Flour and Bread reference (1977). The supply of flour and bread in the United Kingdom was referred to the MMC for an investigation as to whether a monopoly situation existed, and if so, were any steps taken to exploit the monopoly situation against the public interest. The Commission reported that the market was dominated by three large firms, Associated British Foods Limited, Spillers Limited and Rank Hovis McDougall Limited. None of these three producers individually accounted for more than 33 per cent of the market (the required figure is now 25 per cent), so a structural monopoly situation did not exist. The MMC found, though, that a complex monopoly situation existed in respect of the supply of flour because each of the three major groups required its flour-using subsidiaries to buy their flour from the group's own mills. This meant that over 50 per cent of the market for flour was closed to competition from other flour suppliers. The three groups were so conducting their affairs so as to prevent or restrict competition. A monopoly situation thus existed because of the behaviour of the dominant firms in the market.

The market

A monopoly situation can only be defined by reference to the relevant market. In a sense every supplier of goods is a monopoly if the market is defined narrowly enough, and therefore what constitutes the market is a question of fact in each case. It is necessary to look at the nature of the goods or services themselves, the geographical area in which they are supplied, and also the question of time.

In looking at the nature of the goods or services supplied, consideration should be paid to the availability of substitutes. Put simply, the higher the cross elasticity of demand, the more difficult it will be to show that a supplier is in a dominant market position, as purchasers will turn to substitutes if the price for a product rises too far or supply is restricted. A low cross elasticity of demand means that purchasers are unable or unwilling to turn to substitutes, which means that the supplier is in a stronger market position than one where substitutes are readily available.

Many producers attempt to promote brand loyalty, thus reducing the cross elasticity of demand for their products. The more successful they are in doing this may mean that they are more likely to be in a dominant market position, and thus more likely to come under the scrutiny of the MMC. By encouraging and promoting brand loyalty, purchasers may prefer to pay a higher price rather than turn to substitutes.

Consider, for example, the market for bananas. Is this a market in itself, or part of the wider market for fruit? A supplier may have control over, say, 90 per cent of the market for bananas in the United Kingdom, but this market may form only a tiny percentage of the wider fruit market. The supplier will be a monopolist if the market is defined in terms of bananas, but not if defined in terms of fruit. This depends on the cross elasticity of demand between bananas and other fruit.

The identity of the market was once an important feature of a monopoly investigation. Under the 1973 Act, however, the criteria for deciding which goods are to be considered by the MMC in their investigation are to be determined by the reference itself. This is provided in section 10 (7) which states that the person who makes the reference, that is the Director or secretary of state, shall determine the criteria as to which goods or services shall be included in the reference. Thus in the Ready Mixed Concrete reference of 1979, the Director defined for the purpose of the reference the goods as follows:

(a) Concrete means any substance consisting predominantly of a mixture of sand, stone, cement and water, and

(b) 'ready-mixed' means mixed to a fresh condition . . .

elsewhere than at the site where the concrete is required for use.

The person making the reference may also, as well as defining the goods or services which are to be referred, define the parties to whom or by whom the goods are supplied, or the places where they are supplied. In the Roadside Advertising reference (1979) the reference defined the services as advertisements on sites of not less than 40 inches wide and 60 inches deep which are visible from a highway, including a pedestrian precinct, but excluding sites on any form of conveyance. And in the Holiday Caravans in Northern Ireland reference (1981) the reference was limited to the supply of the service by licence holders.

The second important ingredient of the market is the geographical area. A person may be in a monopoly situation if the geographical area is narrowly defined, but not if a wider area is taken. The relevant market, except of course in monopoly situations in relation to exports, is stated by the Act to be the United Kingdom. Section 9, however, allows the reference to be limited to a part of the United Kingdom, and if this is done, the Commission must restrict its investigation to the area as limited by the reference. If there is no such limitation, then the Commission must look at the whole of the United Kingdom market. In the Holiday Caravans reference above, the area was limited to Northern Ireland, and in the investigation into London postal services, the area was defined as the numbered London Postal Districts.

The third factor in determining the relevant market is that of time. If, for example, a householder has a burst pipe, and all the plumbers in the area, except one, are fully booked and cannot do the repair, the one plumber who is available is in a monopoly situation, though only temporarily. Similarly, the Gas Board, in attempting to market heating systems, will face competition from other energy suppliers. Once a customer has installed a gas heating system, the Gas Board may be in a monopoly situation, as a change to other systems is unlikely to be an economic proposition. The cross elasticity of demand is high in the initial marketing, but low once a heating system has been installed.

Monopoly references

The power to make a monopoly reference is vested in both the Director and the secretary of state. In practice it is invariably the Director who makes the reference, unless he is precluded by the Act from making a reference. The power of the Director to make a reference is contained in section 50, but he cannot do so in relation to goods and services listed in Schedule 5 and Schedule 7, part 1. These include the supply of gas, electricity, road and rail services, water, postal services and port facilities. In these cases the reference must be made by the secretary of state, whose powers under section 51 are generally unlimited. The secretary can also veto a reference made by the Director, but his power of veto is unlikely to be used. The purpose of granting powers of reference to the Director was to take many references out of the political arena, and if the secretary of state did exercise a veto, he would have to state his reasons and justify himself in the House of Commons.

Both sections 50 and 51 state that a reference may be made as the Director or secretary of state think fit. There is no duty to make a reference.

Types of reference

A monopoly reference can either be limited to the facts, or can be a public interest reference. The distinction is important, because if a reference is limited to the facts, then the secretary of state has no power to make any order. Every reference must, by section 47, specify:

(1) the description of the goods or services to which it relates;
(2) if it relates to goods, whether it relates to the supply of goods in the United Kingdom or to exports from the United Kingdom; and
(3) the part of the United Kingdom to which the reference relates, if so limited.

The reference may also direct the MMC to exclude certain agreements or practices from the investigation.

A reference which is limited to the facts is made under section 48. It requires the MMC to limit itself in the investigation to purely factual matters. The questions the MMC must consider are:

(1) whether a monopoly situation exists and of what type;
(2) in whose favour the monopoly situation exists;
(3) whether any steps are being taken to exploit or maintain the monopoly situation; and
(4) whether any act or omission is attributable to the existence of the monopoly situation.

The MMC is precluded from considering whether any of the steps taken to exploit, or maintain, the monopoly situation are against the public interest, and from making any recommendations.

Very few references are limited to the facts, and invariably the MMC is asked to make a public interest investigation under section 49. A reference under this section covers all the points of a factual reference, but in addition requires the MMC to consider whether any facts found in pursuance of the investigation operate or may be expected to operate against the public interest. However, the MMC may be required to confine its investigation to those steps taken by the dominant firm or firms which are specified in the reference. This procedure saves the MMC time in not having to investigate whether the monopoly situation as a whole operates against the public interest, by restricting the reference to certain practices. Thus in the Breakfast Cereals reference, 1973, the reference was restricted to the determination of price levels.

Section 78 of the Act also allows the secretary of state to make a general reference, by asking the MMC to consider and report on the effect on the public interest of specified practices which are commonly adopted as a result of, or for the purpose of preserving monopoly situations, and specified practices which appear to be uncompetitive ones. The Commission may also be asked to report on the desirability of any action for the purpose of remedying or preventing effects adverse to the public interest. References under this section can only be made by the secretary of state and not the Director.

Although the MMC has made several reports on general references, very few have led to legislation to control the practice. However, the first general reference, that relating to collective price discrimination, did lead to legislation, the practice being made illegal in the 1956 Restrictive Trade Practices Act.

Monopoly reports

The general duty of investigating and reporting on questions referred to the MMC is laid down in section 5, and the report itself must comply with the requirements of section 54. When the MMC makes its report, it must include definite conclusions on the questions comprised in the reference, give reasons for those conclusions and survey the general position with respect to the subject matter of the reference. Where the reference is not limited to the facts, and the MMC finds that a monopoly situation both exists, and operates against the public interest, the report must further specify the effects contrary to the public interest. It must then consider what action should be taken to remedy or prevent those adverse effects, and may include in its report recommendations as to such action.

Subsequent action

Action can only be taken on a monopoly report when it is a public interest reference, and not when it is one limited to the facts. Four other pre-conditions are required by section 56 (1). These are that the report must have been laid before Parliament; the MMC must have concluded that a monopoly situation exists; the conclusion of the MMC must be that the facts found operate or may be expected to operate against the public interest; and the conclusions must specify the particular effects which are adverse to the public interest. Provided that the report complies with section 56 (1), informal or formal action can follow.

Informal action

Provision is made by section 88 for the Director to consult with the relevant parties with a view to obtaining undertakings from them. The Director can only act on a request from the appropriate minister, and the undertaking which the Director secures is given to the minister and not the Director. The Director is charged with keeping the situation under review to see that the undertaking is being complied with, or needs modification. If the undertaking is being broken, or modification is required, then the Director will advise the minister. If an undertaking is not forthcoming, the Director advises the minister regarding the making of an order.

Formal action

The powers of the appropriate minister to make an order are contained in section 56 (2). He may, by an order made by a statutory instrument, exercise one or more of the powers specified in Schedule 8 of the Act, as he considers fit, for the purpose of remedying the adverse effects specified in the report of the MMC. The minister must take account of the recommendations made by the MMC and any advice given by the Director, but he is not bound to follow these recommendations or advice, and in fact he is under no compulsion to make any order at all.

The power contained in Schedule 8 is divided into two parts. Part I includes the power to prohibit the carrying out of agreements, the withholding of supplies, discrimination, or tying-terms. The minister can compel the publication and notification of prices, and he also has the power to control prices. Part II provides powers for the division of the business or divestment. The powers of the minister are more restricted in this case as they cannot be exercised in the case of statutory bodies, and before any order comes into effect it must be approved by a resolution in both Houses of Parliament. In the Domestic Gas Appliance reference published in 1980, the MMC found that the gas appliance retailing monopoly of the British Gas Corporation operated against the public interest. It put forward two options to remedy the situation. Either the Corporation should abandon certain practices, such as price discrimination in its favour from the appliance manufacturers, or it should discontinue its retailing function. As the British Gas Corporation is a statutory body, the minister does not have the power to order the divestment recommended. Hence when the minister announced in Parliament that the Corporation would be required to cease selling appliances, and sell its showrooms, she announced that legislation would be introduced to compel this. An order under section 56 would not be sufficient.

Enforcement

The breach of an undertaking does not lead to any legal sanction, though the minister could impose an order based on the original report of the MMC. However, such a breach is very unlikely, as most undertakings will have been entered into after discussions and negotiations with the Director, and in any case, to be accused of breaching an undertaking is not a good advertisement for the firm concerned.

The breach of an order can lead to legal sanctions, but is not a criminal offence, enforcement being by civil procedure. The Crown, under section 93 (2), can seek an injunction or other appropriate relief against any person who contravenes an order. Failure to comply with a court order would be contempt of court, punishable by a fine or imprisonment.

It is not clear whether an individual harmed by a breach could seek an injunction or compensation. Section 93 (2) seems to suggest that this is the case, though the matter has not yet been tested. The action would be for breach of statutory duty, and any individual who sought damages would have to show that he has sufficient interest, and that he is one of those whom the order was intended to protect. As most orders are made to protect the general public interest this would be a difficult hurdle to overcome. For the breach of some orders, e.g. not to discriminate, a person who was still discriminated against would, it is presumed, have sufficient interest to litigate.

Appeals

Another question on which there is some doubt is whether a person against whom an order is made can appeal against it. Presumably a right of appeal would exist on procedural grounds, that is if the minister had not followed the correct procedure before making an order. Also an order would be *ultra vires* if the preconditions required by section 56 (1) were not complied with. It is not clear, however, whether the MMC, in conducting an investigation, is bound by the rules of natural justice.

One of the few cases to come before the courts was *Hoffman la Roche A. G. v Secretary of State for Trade and Industry (1974)* which concerned the order controlling the prices that Roche Products could charge for their drugs, librium and valium. Roche held a patent for the two drugs and a MMC report found that the prices charged were excessive and should be substantially reduced. The secretary of state made an order reducing the price of the drugs by 40 per cent and 25 per cent respectively, the order being approved by both Houses of Parliament. Roche claimed that the order was invalid on the grounds that the MMC in its investigation failed to observe the rules of natural justice, and that the report on which the order was based, was void. They stated that they would disregard the order, and restore the prices of librium and valium to their original level, but would pay the difference in prices into a bank account to await a decision of the courts as to the validity of the order. They issued a writ against the secretary of state claiming a declaration that the order was invalid because it was made *ultra vires*. The secretary of state issued a writ claiming an interim injunction, pending a hearing of the substantive issue, restraining Roche from charging prices in excess of those specified by the order. Roche were prepared to submit to the interim injunction provided that an undertaking was given that if the order was subsequently held to be unvalid, the Crown would compensate them for the losses incurred in charging the lower prices. The House of Lords, confirming the decision of the Court of Appeal, held that the order was *intra vires* on the face of it, and the secretary of state was entitled to an interim injunction without being required to give an undertaking in respect of damages.

The question as to whether the MMC is bound by the rules of natural justice was not necessary to this decision, and the substantive case was not brought. In the Court of Appeal, Lord Denning did consider the question of natural justice. He stated that if the MMC had acted contrary to natural justice, the report would not be void, and that:

> A failure to observe the rules of natural justice does not render a decision, order, or report absolutely void in the sense that it is a nullity. . . . A person who has been unfairly treated . . . can go to the courts . . . for a declaration that it is invalid, that it has not and never has had, any effect against him. But it is a personal remedy, personal to him. . . .
> So here the report of the Monopolies Commission even if made in breach of the rules of natural justice is still capable of legal consequences.

The secretary of state was therefore entitled to treat the report as valid, and the order he made which was based on the report, was also valid. To attack the MMC for want of natural justice, Roche would have had to take steps to have the report declared invalid before the order was made, as the court would have the power to restrain steps taken to implement an invalid report. The question, however, as to whether the MMC is bound by the rules of natural justice is still unanswered.

Public interest

When the MMC is asked to consider the effect on the public interest of a monopoly situation, an important factor is the definition of the public interest. The guidelines to what is or is not in the public interest are laid down in section 84. This provides that:

> In determining for any purposes . . . whether any particular matter operates, or may be expected to operate, against the public interest the MMC shall take into account all matters which appear to them in the particular circum-

stances to be relevant, and among other things, shall have regard to the desirability —

(a) of maintaining and promoting effective competition between persons supplying goods and services in the United Kingdom;
(b) of promoting the interests of consumers, purchasers and other users of goods and services in the United Kingdom in respect of the prices charged for them and in respect of their quality and the variety of goods and services supplied;
(c) of promoting, through competition, the reduction of costs and the development and use of new techniques and new products, and of facilitating the entry of new competitors into existing markets;
(d) of maintaining and promoting the balance distribution of industry and employment in the United Kingdom;
(e) of maintaining and promoting competitive activity in markets outside the United Kingdom on the part of producers of goods, and of suppliers of goods and services, in the United Kingdom.

The emphasis in section 84 is clearly on the desirability of competition, and the interests of the consumer, purchaser and user of goods and services. The matters laid down are not exclusive, but merely guidelines to the MMC, who can take into account all relevant matters. The MMC, under section 84, is not absolutely bound, but 'shall have regard to the desirability of . . .', and it is free to take its own decisions. This allows the MMC to follow a flexible, non-rigid approach.

Barriers to entry

In practice, the MMC has rarely condemned a monopoly situation unless steps have been taken to keep other firms out of the market. In order to make monopoly profits in the long run, it is necessary to provide barriers in order to prevent competitors entering the market. Without such barriers, the existence of excess profits will attract new entrants. So it is where a firm has used its dominant position to restrict new entrants and preserve its monopoly position that the Commission has been most critical. It is not the dominant position as such that is condemned, but the steps taken to preserve and exploit it.

One of the ways in which a dominant position has been preserved is by discriminatory and predatory pricing. This practice has been universally condemned by the MMC. Two references in which this practice was found to exist were the Match reference (1973) and the Industrial and Medicinal Gases reference (1956). The British Match Co. had almost complete monopoly of the market for matches, and effectively kept out competition by temporary price cuts whenever anyone tried to enter the market. British Oxygen supplied over 90 per cent of the market for oxygen, and used 'fighting' companies, that is subsidiaries which it was not known to control, to compete at very low prices, in areas where another firm tried to enter the market. The MMC condemned both companies, and undertakings were entered into.

The appointment of sole distributors has been condemned in certain instances where it has inhibited competition and made it difficult for competitors to enter the market. In the Clutches reference (1968), it was found that Automotive Products had a network of appointed dealers who were contracted to handle only their products. The effect of this was to restrain competition in general, and in particular made it difficult for one of its smaller competitors to compete. This firm was in fact forced to establish its own chain of distributors in order to sell its products. The MMC recommended that Automotive Products should abandon its exclusive dealing clauses and undertakings were given.

One interesting case was the Household Detergents reference, (1966). The report showed that over 90 per cent of household detergents were supplied by two firms, Unilever and Procter & Gamble. The MMC objected to the fact that the advertising and promotion costs totalled about 25 per cent of the retail price. The high promotion costs made it difficult for other, smaller firms to compete, as these costs for them would be disproportionately high. New firms were thus effectively kept out of the market by this practice.

It was recommended that these promotional costs should be reduced by 40 per cent. This would make it easier for other firms to enter the market, increase competition and enable the two larger firms to compete against each other on prices, thus reducing prices to the consumer. Appropriate undertakings were given. Unilever and Procter & Gamble were released from these undertakings in 1981 as significant changes had been seen in the detergents market, including new products, the emergence of an additional supplier with over 10 per cent of the market and the growing purchasing power of large retailers, who often marketed their own brands.

Merely because a monopoly is following a course of conduct which has the effect of keeping others out of the market, does not necessarily mean that it is automatically contrary to the public interest. In the Bread and Flour reference the practice of requiring subsidiaries to buy flour from the groups' own mills closed over 50 per cent of the market to others and restrained entry. But the MMC concluded that this practice did not operate against the public interest. The fact that a dominant firm has expanded its plant in order to meet expected future demand, thus making it unprofitable for new firms to compete, has been welcomed by the MMC. In fact the MMC has criticized firms for not developing new capacity to meet future demand.

Conclusion

The control of Monopoly in the United Kingdom is by administrative rather than legal process. Monopolies are not condemned *per se*, and the machinery under the Act is based on a pragmatic case by case approach. What is condemned is the abuse of monopoly power where this leads to the interests of the public being adversely affected. Monopoly is not presumed to be against the public interest as is the case with restrictive trading agreements. The MMC has to say whether the steps taken to exploit or maintain a dominant position operate or can be expected to operate against the public interest. It is not for those in whose favour a monopoly situation exists to show that it is in the public interest.

It has been said that in the United Kingdom, a strong line against monopoly and dominant positions is not taken. As has been seen, it is not illegal for a monopoly to abuse its position by charging high prices, discriminating, keeping others out of the market, refusing to supply or imposing other anti-competitive practices, unless there has been a monopoly report by a ministerial order. Monopoly investigations are often lengthy and there is a limitation on the number of investigations which the MMC can carry out, perhaps four of five per year. It may therefore be a long time, even years, before an abuse of a monopoly position has been referred, reported on and an order made. It seems there is some argument for moving towards the continental approach, which while not condemning monopoly as such, does make unlawful the abuse of a dominant position. The Liesner Report on Monopolies and Mergers Policy (Liesner, 1978) however, favours the less legalistic and more pragmatic United Kingdom approach, and states that many countries who have adopted a judicial approach are tending to move towards a more pragmatic policy.

The Report did, however, state that some sectors of the economy are dominated by a very few large firms, which give rise to some worries about economic power, and certain practices of some dominant firms are directly aimed at restricting competition. These forms of behaviour were said to be unsuited to case by case investigation, and could be dealt with on a more general basis. This could take the form of making unlawful certain types of anti-competitive practice, in the same way that collective refusal to supply is unlawful under the Restrictive Trade Practices Act, 1976. The Report did however recommend that the definition of a monopoly situation in relation to oligopoly should be on a structural basis, rather than at present, on a behavioural one.

Some of the problems may be alleviated by the Competition Act 1980 (see Chapter 4) which provides a simplified procedure for investigating anti-competitive practices. Under this Act there is no need to establish that a monopoly situation exists; an investigation of the whole of the market to assess market share is not relevant; and the Director has the power to extract an undertaking without making a reference. Many situations which would have required a full monopoly reference are being dealt with under this Act. Nevertheless, there is still a strong suspicion that monopoly control is not being exercised with all the rigour which is possible.

4

Anti-competitive Practices

Introduction

The provisions of the Competition Act 1980 in relation to anti-competitive practices are intended to complement those of the Fair Trading Act, and allow the investigation of practices of single firms which restrict, distort or prevent competition. Under the Fair Trading Act, the Director has the duty of collecting information about, and keeping under review commercial activities which relate to monopoly situations and uncompetitive practices. However, the Director can only take action under the Act where he suspects that a monopoly situation exists. Under the Competition Act, the Director can take action against a single firm where there is no monopoly situation.

A monopoly reference has several limitations. No action can be taken by the Director himself; he can only make a reference to the MMC, though the mere threat of a reference can persuade a firm to end its anti-competitive behaviour. The investigation can only deal with the practices of a firm which turns out to be a monopolist, that is, more than 25 per cent of the market. This therefore means that a complete market sector must be investigated, and extend to all firms within that sector, not just to the practices of a single firm suspected of engaging in uncompetitive behaviour. This investigation, and the impact of the various trading practices of the firms concerned on the public interest, can be a time-consuming process, and a monopoly investigation can last some years.

The Competition Act provides for a similar sort of

procedure to a monopoly investigation, but it is much simpler and quicker. A two-stage approach is adopted. The Director himself, if he believes a firm is engaging in a course of conduct which may amount to an anti-competitive practice, can make an investigation. Only if a firm refuses to give a satisfactory undertaking to the Director following an investigation can the Director make a competition reference to the MMC. The Director is not concerned with whether the course of conduct is contrary to the public interest, but merely whether it adversely affects competition.

Where a reference is made, the MMC are required to report on whether the course of conduct is anti-competitive, and if so, whether it is contrary to the public interest. Following an adverse report, the secretary of state can make an order either prohibiting the practice, or remedying its adverse effects. Alternatively, he can ask the Director to seek an undertaking from the firm concerned. There are time limits given in the Act at all stages in the procedure, so as to speed up the process of investigation.

Anti-competitive practices

Definition

An anti-competitive practice is defined in section 2 (1) of the Act as one where in the course of a business, a person

> pursues a course of conduct which, of itself or when taken together with a course of conduct pursued by persons associated with him, has or is intended to have or is likely to have the effect of restricting, distorting or preventing competition in connection with the production, supply or acquisition of goods in the United Kingdom or any part of it or the supply or securing of services in the United Kingdom or any part of it.

The Act does not contain any list of practices which are deemed to be, or likely to be, anti-competitive. A generalist approach is adopted, and any course of conduct can amount to an anti-competitive practice if there is a restriction, distortion or prevention of competition. This flexible approach allows each course of conduct to be individually investigated, with consideration being given to all the circumstances which may be relevant in a particular case. Practices are thus assessed by reference to their effects on competition, as in Common Market legislation, rather than by reference to their form, as with the United Kingdom restrictive practices legislation.

Although the Act makes no mention of monopoly or dominant market position, it is more likely, in practice, that a firm with some market power will be more able to affect competition by its activities than firms with little or no market power. Small firms who do not enjoy a degree of market power are unlikely to be the subject of an investigation. This is one of the reasons for the adoption of a flexible approach, and not classifying which practices are likely to be anti-competitive. In the Parliamentary debates, a government spokesman, after giving some examples of possible anti-competitive practices, but stressing that the list was not comprehensive, went on to say:

> Further, as I have stressed before, the practices are not necessarily anti-competitive; for example, when employed by a small firm fighting for entry to a market. One of the main consderations will be the degree of market power the firm enjoys. (HL Deb., vol. 406, col. 64)

Although a full market analysis will not be necessary, as in a monopoly reference, it will be important to identify the market in which a firm operates in order to assess the degree of market power the firm enjoys.

One limitation on the generality of the definition of an anti-competitive practice is that there must be a course of conduct. Therefore a single, isolated act is not caught. The course of conduct must be in the course of a business. One exception to this is given in section 2 (8). Where a local authority pursues a course of conduct in connection with the acquisition of goods or the securing of services by it, it is not necessary to show that the local authority was acting in the course of a business.

An anti-competitive practice can be carried out by a local

authority in the course of any of its activities, except those relating to the supply of goods or services free of charge. However, although the purchasing activities are included, the government made it clear during the passage of the legislation through Parliament, that there was no intention of interfering with the practice of selective competitive tendering, because of the benefits of this system both to local authorities and their suppliers. The activities of nationalized industries can also be investigated, and in fact, three investigations have been made so far into the practices of British Rail.

Exclusions

Section 2 (3) gives the power to the secretary of state to exclude certain courses of conduct from constituting anticompetitive practices either by reference to a particular class of person, or to particular circumstances, and section 2 (4) states that this can include a person by reference to the size of the business. A limited number of exclusions have been made by the Anti-Competitive Practices (Exclusions) Order (1980).

One exclusion relates to the activities of small firms, who are unlikely to be able to affect competition to any material extent, and it would be a waste of the limited resources of the Office of Fair Trading to make investigations into these activities. The Order exempts from the definition of anticompetitive practices the activities of firms who have a turnover of £5 million of less, or a share of the relevant market of 25 per cent or less, and who are not members of a group of companies exceeding those figures. Whether an investigation could be made of a firm with less than £5 million turnover will, to a certain extent, depend on how the market is defined. If defined narrowly enough, in relation both to the product and geographical area, presumably quite small firms could be investigated.

The Order also excludes certain courses of conduct. These include practices relating to the supply of goods outside the United Kingdom, and the activities of certain specified sectors including international aviation and shipping, and the provision of public transport by local authorities.

Section 2 (2) of the Act also excludes any course of conduct arising from a material part of an agreement registrable under the restrictive practices legislation.

Affecting competition

The course of conduct must be such as that it 'has or is intended to have or is likely to have the effect of restricting, distorting or preventing competition'. Thus there are three different possibilities for investigation. The practice may actually have an effect on competition, even though there was no such intention. In this case, some form of market analysis will be necessary, in order to discover what the consequences of the course of conduct are. Similarly, where the conduct is likely to affect competition in the future. However, a course of conduct is still anti-competitive, even though it does not affect, or is incapable of affecting, competition, if that is the intention of the firm by engaging in the practice.

The course of conduct must be anti-competitive, and it is not sufficient to show that it is merely against the public interest. Thus monopoly pricing, which is charging a price higher than would be possible in a competitive market, would appear not to be an anti-competitive practice as it does not, and is not intended to, affect competition, even though it may be against the public interest. To curb this sort of practice will still require a full monopoly reference, though it may be an abuse of a dominant market position under Article 86 of the EEC Treaty.

One problem with the definition, raised by Cunningham (1980), is that for competition to be affected, there must be some existing competition. Thus, if a supplier refuses to supply a distributor who is not already in the market, then this cannot restrict, distort, or prevent competition as there is no competition to be restricted, distorted, or prevented. However, it has the effect of preventing potential competition and places a barrier to entry into the market. Erecting barriers to market entry has been the subject of many adverse reports following a monopoly reference, and it is unlikely that the Director will place too restrictive a legalistic definition in making an investigation.

Investigation by the Director

Section 3 (1) gives the Director the power to make an investigation with a view to establishing whether a firm has been, or is pursuing, a course of conduct which amounts to an anti-competitive practice, if such appears to be the case. The jurisdiction of the Director is exclusive, and the secretary of state cannot require the Director to make an investigation, nor can he make a competition reference to the MMC. This contrasts with the position under the Fair Trading Act, where the power to make a monopoly reference is vested in both the Director and the secretary of state.

Most investigations will stem from complaints received by the Office of Fair Trading from persons and firms who complain that they are being affected by a suspected anti-competitive practice, for example discriminatory pricing or a refusal to supply. The Director also has a duty, as has been seen, to collect information about, and keep under review, commercial situations relating to uncompetitive practices, and some investigations will stem from these studies. Before commencing an investigation, the Office will make preliminary enquiries to see if there is any evidence to support a complaint, and will often try to come to some arrangement with the firm involved, so that a formal investigation will not be necessary.

The Director is required, under section 3 (2), prior to an investigation, to give notice to the person whose conduct is to be investigated, notify the secretary of state and publish details of the proposed investigation. Although the secretary of state cannot initiate an investigation, he has, under section 2 (5), the power to veto one, provided he does so within 2 weeks of receiving notice. This power of veto is likely to be used sparingly, and only in exceptional circumstances, such as where a monopoly reference has already been made. The Director has similar powers to acquire information as those under the Fair Trading Act in relation to monopoly references.

Section 3 (10) requires the Director to publish a report as soon as is practicable after completion of the investigation. This report must state, with reasons, whether in his opinion any course of conduct constitutes an anti-competitive practice, and if so, the report must:

(1) specify the person or persons concerned;
(2) specify the goods or services in question; and
(3) state whether he considers it appropriate for him to make a competition reference to the MMC.

If the Director concludes that a course of conduct does not amount to an anti-competitive practice, or if so, a competition reference is not appropriate, then no further action can be taken. Where a reference is considered appropriate, section 4 gives the Director the authority to consider representations from the firm concerned with a view to accepting an undertaking. If an undertaking is given and accepted, the Director is under a duty to monitor the behaviour of the firm, and if it appears that the undertaking has been broken, he can give notice to the firm that he intends to make a reference.

Competition reference

Reference to the MMC

If an undertaking is not given, is not acceptable, or is broken, then the Director can make a competition reference. The reference must be made within the time limited laid down, which are between 4 and 8 weeks (12 with the consent of the secretary of state) from the date of the report, or the date that the Director serves notice on a firm for breach of an undertaking, as the case may be. If a reference is not made within the time limited, the proceedings lapse.

Under section 6 (1) a competition reference must specify:

(1) the person or persons whose activities are to be investigated by the MMC;
(2) the goods or services to which the investigation is to extend; and
(3) the course of conduct to be investigated.

A competition reference must be published, and notice given to the secretary of state, who can direct the Director not to proceed. The MMC must make their report within the time stipulated by the Director, which cannot exceed 6 months.

The MMC must investigate the following matters:

(1)   whether at any time during the previous 12 months, any firm mentioned in the reference was pursuing a specified course of conduct;
(2)   whether that course of conduct amounts to an anti-competitive practice; and
(3)   if so, whether it operates, or might it be expected to operate against the public interest.

In deciding whether a practice is contrary to the public interest, the MMC is required to be guided by section 84 of the Fair Trading Act (see Chapter 3).

Unlike the report of the Director of an investigation, where all he is concerned with is whether the practice is anti-competitive, the MMC has to report whether it is also contrary to the public interest. Thus before the MMC makes an adverse report, there are two questions to be answered. Is the practice anti-competitive, and is it also against the public interest? This therefore allows certain courses of conduct, which may have some restraint on competition, to be allowed to continue if they have some positive benefits to the public, or even if they are neutral in that respect. A refusal to supply may be anti-competitive, but it may be to the advantage of consumers if the refusal to supply relates to certain criteria, such as after-sales service, specialist advice, or keeping spare parts available in stock.

Report of the MMC

The report of the MMC, which is made to the secretary of state, must include their conclusions on the matter put to them. If they conclude that there is no course of conduct amounting to an anti-competitive practice, or if so, it is not contrary to the public interest, then no action can be taken. If the report concludes that there is an anti-competitive course of conduct which is against the public interest, the report must specify the adverse effects, and it may make recommendations about the action to be taken to remedy these effects.

There is no duty for any action to be taken following an adverse report. If action is taken then it can be formal or informal, similar to that following an adverse monopoly report. Thus, the secretary of state can ask the Director to seek an undertaking from the firm concerned, which the Director will keep under review. Failing a satisfactory undertaking, the secretary of state can make an Order prohibiting the named person or persons from engaging in specified anti-competitive activity, or in a course of conduct similar in effect. In addition, the secretary of state can exercise any of the powers available following a monopoly reference, as specified in Schedule 8 of the Fair Trading Act.

Types of anti-competitive practices

The Act, as has been noted, does not contain any list or guidance as to the types of practice which are anti-competitive. The Office of Fair Trading has, however, published a guide to the Act, in which are indicated the type of practices which are likely to be anti-competitive. These practices will not always be anti-competitive, and much will depend on the circumstances, but nevertheless the guide provides a useful indication to business of the types of conduct which are likely to attract the attention of the Director. Further guidance can be obtained from the published reports of the MMC with regard to monopoly references, which provide pointers to the types of practice which in the past, have been condemned, but it should be pointed out that the prime concern of a monopoly report is the effect on the public interest and not on competition.

Anti-competitive practices are likely to fall within three main categories, those relating to pricing policy, those relating to distribution policy, and refusals to supply.

Pricing policy

Discriminatory and predatory pricing are practices which are likely to attract the attention of the Director as being anti-competitive practices. Discriminatory pricing, the practice of charging different prices to distinct and separate customers which do not reflect differences in the costs of supply, can favour a powerful buyer, and strengthen his competitive position in the market in which he is selling. The MMC, in its Report on Discounts to Retailers (1981), looked at the question of supplying goods to certain retailers, where prices did not reflect the cost saving on large transactions. Although the MMC considered that generally the practice was not against the public interest, and that cost savings were, at least in part, passed on to consumers, in some instances, cases of price discrimination could be anti-competitive and against the public interest. The MMC thought that it would be appropriate to make an investigation under the Act in certain cases.

The practice, which is now the subject of an inquiry by the Office of Fair Trading, of certain large buyers unfairly squeezing producers to obtain larger discounts, could also be an anti-competitive practice, and be the subject of an investigation.

Predatory pricing, the practice of charging temporarily low prices, often below cost, with the intention of preventing or eliminating competition, has been condemned by both the MMC and the EC Commission. The behaviour of British Oxygen (Reference on Industrial and Medical Gases, 1956) in lowering their prices in certain parts of the country was held by the MMC to be anti-competitive, as it created barriers to entry into the market. Predatory pricing was held by the EC Commission in *AKZO (1983)* (see Chapter 5) to be an abuse of a dominant position within the Common Market, because of the attempt to restrict or prevent competition.

Vertical price squeezing is another activity relating to pricing policies which could be anti-competitive. This arises when a vertically integrated firm is in a strong market position in relation to a product essential to the production requirements of both an associate company and its competitors. The integrated firm can charge a high price for this product, but a low output price, thus squeezing the profits of its competitors. The practice was found to be against the public interest in the Monopoly Reference on Man Made Fibres (1968), where Courtaulds gave an undertaking not to discriminate between its own subsidiaries and their competitors.

One of the earliest investigations under the Competition Act in relation to pricing policy occurred in the investigation into the London Electricity Board (1982). The Director reported that the practice of the Board in carrying on the retail side of the business at a loss over a period of at least 5 years, failing to charge prices which reflected costs and offsetting these losses against the more profitable business of supplying electricity, where it is a monopoly supplier, was unfair to its competitors. The course of conduct constituted, in the opinion of the Director, an anti-competitive practice, and he has made a competition reference to the Commission.

Distribution

The Office of Fair Trading have identified several practices in relation to distribution policies, which may restrict, distort or prevent competition, and many have been the subject of monopoly references. One such example is tie-in sales, which refer to a condition that a buyer must purchase a certain quantity of one product in order to be able to purchase quantities of another. In the Report on the Supply of Films (1966), the MMC was of the opinion that this practice was anti-competitive, in that the requirement to make the supply of one film conditional on the supply of others tended to exclude other films which may have been more acceptable to both the exhibitor and the public.

Full line forcing agreements can also be anti-competitive, as these require a buyer to purchase certain quantities of each item in a product range to be able to buy any of them. Competition is restricted in that the buyer cannot seek supplies from elsewhere.

Many competition references are likely to involve exclusive supply, exclusive purchasing and selective distribution agreements. Although some agreements can be in the public interest and actually increase competition, others can have a detrimental effect on competition. An exclusive contract was held by the Director to be an anti-competitive practice in the investigation into British Rail franchising of taxis at Brighton station. Under the arrangement between British Rail and a taxi firm, only that firm's taxis were allowed to use the station forecourt to seek custom, although others could drop passengers there.

Rental only contracts may also attract the Director's attention. These restrict customers to rental or lease terms only, and where there are no alternatives to acquiring the goods, they are anti-competitive. In the monopoly Reference into the Supply of Electrostatic Reprographic Equipment (1976), the MMC took the view that the policy of Rank Xerox in supplying copying machines on a rental only basis, restricted consumer choice and prevented the development of other leasing facilities, particularly in view of the substantial market power enjoyed by Rank Xerox.

Refusal to supply

A consequence of many of the pricing and distribution policies of firms will be a refusal to deal or supply, and so far they have been the subject of the majority of investigations under the Act. Some have related to the refusal to supply low price or discount dealers, a practice which is often suspected of being a 'back door' method of enforcing resale price maintenance.

The investigation into the distribution policies of Raleigh Cycles in 1981 involved a refusal to supply certain retailers. Raleigh laid down certain criteria which dealers had to meet before they would supply cycles for resale. The Director carried out an investigation, and concluded that the refusal to supply dealers who did not meet the criteria was an anti-competitive practice. This refusal, in the opinion of the Director, restricted competition between retailers and deprived consumers of lower prices. A competition reference was made to the MMC, who reported adversely in relation to some of the criteria, which included servicing facilities, commitment to cycle retailing, carrying stocks of spares and geographical area. An undertaking was given to the Director relating to the supply of cycles to discount retailers.

The refusal to supply by Sheffield Newspapers was also the subject of an investigation by the Director. Sheffield Newspapers refused to supply newsagents who stocked and distributed free newspapers, which were in competition, particularly for advertising. It was referred to the MMC who reported that the refusal was an anti-competitive practice which operated against the public interest. It restricted competition between free and paid-for publications as a means of advertising, and between newsagents in that they could not compete in undertaking new business. It was contrary to the public interest because without competition advertising charges were likely to be higher, and consumer choice would be restricted. Further there would be less incentive to maintain standards of service. Following the publication of the report, undertakings were accepted by the Director.

The investigation into the practices of *W. M. Still & Sons Ltd. (1982)* provided an illustration of a refusal to deal and discriminatory pricing. Still & Sons were manufacturers of catering equipment, and they refused to supply spare parts to firms who serviced such equipment. Manufacturers often undertake servicing themselves, but only of their own products. Competition is thus provided by the independent servicing firms, who are able to provide a service across a range of equipment. By refusing to supply, Still were restricting competition between themselves and the independent servicing firms.

The independents, although they could not buy directly from Still, they could obtain supplies from distributors, whom Still supplied with spares. Certain appointed distributors were offered special discounts of between 15 and 20 per cent. If these distributors also carried out servicing on behalf of Still, the discounts placed them at a competitive advantage in relation to the independents. It reduced the independents' ability to compete, and created barriers to entry into the market. The granting of these special discounts thus distorted competition.

A competition reference was not made, as Still gave satisfactory undertakings to the Director. They undertook not to refuse to supply spares for reasons based solely on the category of the customer, and also agreed not to discriminate in the terms of payment between different classes of customer, unless they fully reflected manufacturing or distribution costs.

Conclusion

The Competition Act thus brings under control the practices of single firms were a monopoly situation does not exist, and even where one does exist, the procedure under the Competition Act offers certain advantages. It does not have to be shown that there is a monopoly situation, a full market analysis is not necessary, the Director can make a preliminary investigation himself, and because the Act provides various time limits, investigations are likely to be much quicker. The flexible approach adopted also has advantages compared with the rather precise definitions of restrictive trading agreements.

There must be some doubt, though, whether the Act has any real teeth. In the first place the policing of anti-competitive practice depends on the resources available to the Office of Fair Trading. It was envisaged that the Office would be able to deal with twenty to thirty investigations a year. In practice the number of investigations has been much lower, and in 1982 only two were initiated. The chances of a firm being investigated must be very slight. However, the mere threat of an investigation will encourage many firms to cease various practices in order to avoid the investigation of their affairs, and to avoid adverse publicity.

A second defect is that practices as a whole cannot be condemned, but only the activities of an individual firm. This, of course, is inevitable given the flexible approach adopted, but it can lead to the situation in which the practices of one firm can be prohibited, whilst its competitors are still free to carry on similar practices.

The main criticism, however, is that which applies to most of United Kingdom competition policy, i.e. the lack of adequate sanctions against those who engage in anti-competitive practices. There would appear to be a strong case for having the power to impose fines on those who engage in anti-competitive practices, subject to an appeal, similar to the powers of the EC Commission and the German Karte-lamt. There is also a strong case for imposing civil liability on a firm which engages in practices which are deemed to be anti-competitive. This would, therefore, enable another firm which has suffered damage as a result of the course of conduct of another to be able to seek damages or an injunction.

Nevertheless, the Act is a significant advance in the control of anti-competitive behaviour by firms, as it brings under control several practices not previously caught, in the absence of a monopoly situation. How effective the control is will depend on the Office of Fair Trading and its resources. If only a few investigations can be made each year, the control will be weak, as the chances of a firm being caught will be slim.

5

Dominant Position
Within the EEC

Introduction

In the examination of monopoly control, consideration must
also be given to the EEC rules on competition, which form
part of the law of the United Kingdom. The objects of the
EEC, contained in Article 3 of the EEC Treaty, include 'the
institution of a system ensuring that competition in the
Common Market is not distorted. . . .'

The fundamental provisions are found in the Treaty itself.
Article 85 deals with cartels, while Article 86 is concerned with
the abuse of a dominant position. Article 87 requires the adoption of implementing legislation to give effect to the principles
set out in the Treaty, the most important of which is
Regulation 17, adopted in 1962. The EC Commission, as
guardians of the Treaty, have the duty of seeing that the
competition rules of the Treaty are complied with, and are
given the power to make decisions, which are subject to an
appeal to the European Court of Justice (ECJ). Common
Market competition law is also applied by the national courts
of the Member States.

Articles 85 and 86 are complementary to each other, in that
they are both intended to achieve the same aims, that is to
secure fair competition by curbing restrictive practices.
Article 85 will be considered in detail later (see Chapter 8),
while this chapter considers primarily Article 86, although
there is considerable overlap, and the decisions of the
Commission and the Court are often relevant in the
interpretation of both Articles.

Article 86

Article 86 is concerned with the concentration of economic power, and like the Fair Trading Act in respect of United Kingdom monopoly situations, it condemns the abuse of, rather than the existence of, economic power.

The Article provides that:

Any abuse of a dominant position within the Common Market or in a substantial part of it shall be prohibited as incompatible with the Common Market in so far as it may affect trade between Member States. Such abuse may, in particular, consist in:

(a) directly or indirectly imposing unfair purchase or selling prices or other unfair trading conditions;
(b) limiting production, markets or technical development to the prejudice of consumers;
(c) applying dissimilar conditions to equivalent transactions with other trading parties, thereby placing them at a competitive disadvantage;
(d) making the conclusion of contracts subject to acceptance by the other parties of supplementary obligations which, by their nature or according to commercial usage, have no connection with the subject of such contracts.

It can be seen, therefore, that before Article 86 can be applied, certain conditions must be present. These are:

(1) there must be a dominant position;
(2) within the Common Market, or a substantial part of it;
(3) the dominant position must be abused; and
(4) the abuse must have an effect on trade between Member States.

Dominant position

Unlike the Fair Trading Act, which provides for a market share of 25 per cent before the United Kingdom monopoly legislation can be brought into effect, Article 86 does not require any particular market share. No definition is, in fact, given by the Treaty of a dominant position. It is thus left to the Commission, subject to an appeal to the ECJ, to determine whether or not a dominant position exists by reference to the relevant market factors.

Market share is an important consideration in determining dominance, but it is not the only, or even decisive factor. In *Continental Can Co. Inc. v EC Commission (1972)*, which involved a consideration of whether European subsidiaries of an American company would be in a dominant position after a proposed merger in the metal container market, the ECJ, while giving considerable weight to market share, laid down the test of market dominance as the ability of competitors to constitute an adequate counterweight. In *United Brands v EC Commission (1976)*, where it was held that a market share of 40 per cent of the banana market constituted market dominance, the fact that the largest competitor had a market share of only 9 per cent was an important consideration. Other factors in this case were the high barriers against new entrants to the market, such as penetration costs, access to sources of supply, and the need for large investment.

The concept of market dominance was first examined by the ECJ in *Sirena v Eda (1971)*, where it was defined as the ability or power to prevent effective competition in an important part of the market, considering the position of producers or distributors of similar products. In *Continental Can*, the Commission gave a similar definition, giving as their opinion that undertakings are in a dominant position when they have the power to behave independently, without having to take into account their competitors, purchasers, or suppliers.

In *United Brands*, the ECJ affirmed this opinion of the Commission. They stated that:

a dominant position relates to a position of economic strength enjoyed by an undertaking, which enables it to prevent effective competition being maintained on the relevant market by giving it the power to behave to an appreciable extent independently of its competitors, customers, and ultimately, its consumers.

In *AKZO (1983)*, where a United Kingdom firm complained of predatory and discriminatory pricing by a competitor, the Commission supported a finding of market dominance by reference to the market share of 52 per cent, the relative sizes of the dominant undertaking and its competitors, the commercial and financial strength of the undertaking, and the fact that it was in a position to effectively conduct itself in the manner complained of.

Market dominance must, of course, be considered in relation to the relevant market. What is the relevant market, is also a matter to be determined by the Commission, again subject to an appeal to the ECJ. The relevant market is thus a matter of judicial interpretation. This compares with the position under the Fair Trading Act, where the determination of the relevant market is in the hands of the person making the monopoly reference, that is either the Director General or the minister. The product, and possible substitutes, together with geographical area are important factors in relation to the relevant market.

A good illustration of the principles used to determine the relevant market occurred in *United Brands* (1976). The question for the ECJ was whether the market for bananas was a separate market, or whether it was part of the overall market for fruit. The ECJ considered that for a market to be distinct, it must be sufficiently distinguishable from other markets. It must be possible to single out special factors which make that market separate, so that it is only to a limited extent, if at all, interchangeable with other markets, and only exposed to imperceptible competition. As the ECJ found that bananas were only to a limited extent interchangeable with other fruit, there was a low cross elasticity of demand, and so the market for bananas was quite distinct from the market for other fruit. United Brands were thus in a dominant position.

The same reasoning was applied in *Continental Can*, where the ECJ stated that:

the definition of the relevant market is of essential significance, for the possibility of competition can only be judged in relation to those characteristics of the products . . . which . . . are particularly apt to supply an inelastic need, and only to a limited extent interchangeable with other products.

In this case, the ECJ examined the market for metal cans and containers, but pointed to the existence of other sources of competition, such as containers made of glass or plastic, and the fact that food packers could manufacture their own containers. It thus came to the conclusion that Continental Can were not in a dominant position, as the metal container market was not distinguishable from the market for other food containers.

Within the Common Market

Article 86 requires that an undertaking must be dominant within the Common Market or a substantial part of it, therefore making the geographical area an important factor. The Article does not attempt to define a 'substantial part', again leaving it to the Commission, subject to judicial review, to define this factor, and it is not entirely clear from cases as to how substantial the part must be before it falls within Article 86.

The territory of one Member State has on several occasions been deemed to be sufficiently large to be a substantial part. An undertaking which is therefore dominant in a Member State would appear to be dominant within a substantial part of the Common Market. In *Gema (1971)* and *Continental Can*, Germany was held to be a substantial part of the Common Market, as was the United Kingdom in *AKZO*. In *Garden Cottage Foods Ltd. v Milk Marketing Board (1982)* the Court of Appeal held that England alone was a substantial part of the Common Market, while in *Suiker Unie S.A. v EC Commission (1976)* (the Sugar Cartel case) Holland on its own, and Belgium and Luxembourg taken together, have also been held to be substantial parts.

It is clear from the Sugar Cartel case, that the size of the geographical area is not the sole criterion for determining a substantial part of the Common Market. Attention must also be given to business volume. In the Sugar Cartel case, the ECJ thought that the volume and pattern of production and consumption of the product must be looked at along with geographical area, and in looking at these patterns, together with the size of the area over which the Cartel was dominant, held that it was dominant within a 'substantial part'.

Abuse of a dominant position

Article 86 does not condemn a dominant position in itself, but the improper exploitations of it. The Article gives examples of abuse, which will be prohibited as incompatible with the Common Market. These are:

(1) imposing unfair prices or other trading conditions;
(2) limiting production, markets, or technical development;
(3) discriminating between trading partners; and
(4) imposing obligations in contracts which have no connection with the subject matter of such contracts, e.g. tie-in conditions.

This list of abuses is illustrative and not exhaustive, and it is for the Commission and ECJ to determine, in each individual case, whether the practice or activity complained of is an abuse of a dominant market position.

It is clear from the cases that, although not mentioned in the Article, the abuse of a dominant position must be such that it has a substantial effect on competition. In fact it seems that any form of anti-competitive conduct by a firm in a dominant position will be treated as an abuse. So in *Continental Can*, the ECJ argued that:

> . . . the provision is not only aimed at practices which may cause damage to consumers directly, but also to those which are detrimental to them through their impact on an effective competition structure. . . . Abuse may therefore occur if an undertaking in a dominant position strengthens

such position in a way that the degree of dominance reached substantially fetters competition.

The following have been among the more common types of abuse which have been condemned by the Commission and the ECJ.

Unfair prices

The decisions in *General Motors Continental v EC Commission (1976)* and *United Brands* fall within this category. In *General Motors*, it was said that to charge a price which is excessive in relation to the economic value of a service is an abuse, while in *United Brands* the charging of prices which gave an excessive profit margin was condemned. One test which the ECJ laid down in this case was to ascertain whether the undertaking had made use of its dominant position to reap trading benefits which it would not have reaped if there had been normal and effective competition.

Discriminatory pricing

This is where a different price is charged to different customers, the difference in price not being related to costs. So in *United Brands*, where different prices were charged in different parts of the Common Market, this was treated as an abuse. The ECJ held that price should not be related to what different national markets could bear, but should be related to the costs involved.

Predatory pricing

This is the practice of charging a low price, often below cost, in areas of the market where an undertaking is facing competition, in order to drive out that competition. An example of predatory pricing arose in *AKZO (1983)*. Here, an English firm, ECS, complained to the Commission that AKZO, a Dutch firm, acting through its English subsidiary, approached the major customers of ECS offering to supply at prices considerably less than those offered by ECS, and which ECS could not meet, and also at a price considerably less than those charged by AKZO in other Member States. The intention behind this was to attempt to eliminate ECS from the market, as they were threatening the dominant position of AKZO in other markets, particularly Germany. This was held by the Commission to be an abuse of a dominant position.

Refusal to supply

The refusal to supply goods or services by a firm in a dominant position has invariably been condemned by both the Commission and the ECJ. Thus in *Commercial Solvents Corporation v EC Commission (1974)*, a dominant supplier of a chemical product used in manufacturing, cut off the supply of that product to competitors of one of its subsidiary companies. This was held to be an abuse of a dominant position by the ECJ, as it was an attempt to place its subsidiary in a competitively advantageous position. Another illustration arose in *Garden Cottage Foods Ltd. v Milk Marketing Board (1983)*. GCF purchased butter from the MMB for sale outside the United Kingdom. In 1981, the Board changed their marketing policy. They appointed four distributors to handle bulk supplies of butter for export, and in future, GCF and some fifteen other dealers had to obtain their supplies through these main distributors. GCF took the view that they would be unable to compete profitably on these terms, and sought damages and an injunction for the abuse of a dominant position. Although they did not succeed, and have now made a complaint to the Commission, this failure was on technical grounds of English law. The Court of Appeal, confirmed by the House of Lords, ruled that the Board were in breach of a dominant position within the Common Market.

Unfair trading conditions

This question arose in *Eurofima (1973)*. A buyer of railway stock insisted on inserting in development contracts a term that unlimited patent licences be granted without further remuneration. Although it was conceded that technical co-operation justified the exploitation by the patents of Eurofima for its own needs, the claim that Eurofima could grant these licences to third parties was an abuse of its dominant position.

Affect trade between Member States

The abuse of a dominant position within the Common Market is not subject to Article 86 unless it also affects trade between Member States. In the earlier cases to come before the ECJ it was thought that this meant that there must be some adverse effect on imports and exports between Member States. Recent cases have placed more emphasis on the effect on the competitive structure within the Common Market, than on whether imports and exports are directly affected.

In the *Commercial Solvents* case, where a dominant supplier of raw materials cut off supplies to a former customer, with the aim of eliminating that customer from competing against a subsidiary; Commercial Solvents argued that the effect on inter-community trade would be minimal, as the ex-customer sold over 90 per cent of its output outside the Common Market, and most of the rest in Italy, where it was produced. Further, it would find it difficult to export to other Member States, because this would infringe patents. The Commission held that as it did export a small quantity to other Member States, the effect of the embargo on the supplies of raw material could affect future trade. There was, therefore, an abuse of a dominant position affecting trade between Member States. The ECJ went further than this, when Commercial Solvents appealed against the decision of the Commission. They stated that:

When an undertaking in a dominant position within the Common Market abuses its position in such a way that a competitor in the Common Market is liable to be eliminated, it does not matter whether the conduct relates to the latter's exports or its trade within the Common Market, once it has been established that this elimination will have repercussions on the competitive structure within the Common Market.

In *Vereeniging van Cementhandelaren v EC Commission (1973)*, which involved a breach of Article 85, to which this condition also applies, a trade association recommended the prices at which their members should sell in Holland. It was argued that as this only affected the Dutch market, and did not apply to exports, it did not affect trade between Member States. The ECJ stated that:

> An agreement extending over the whole of the territory of a Member State by its very nature has the effect of compartmentalising of markets on a national basis, thereby holding up the economic interpenetration which the Treaty is designed to bring about. . . .

The ECJ has often repeated the view that the maintenance of separate national markets is contrary to the EEC Treaty, and therefore affects trade between Member States.

The position would seem to be that any agreement or abuse of a dominant position which has the object or effect of significantly restricting competition within any part of the Common Market is likely to be treated as affecting trade between Member States, even if there is no obvious effect on imports and exports between them. This condition, that trade between Member States must be significantly affected, has been referred to frequently by the ECJ as indicating the limits between national and community law. It may well be that, in the light of the pronouncements of the ECJ, this condition is gradually being read out of the Treaty. If this is so, and it has happened in the United States, where the requirement that interstate trade be affected has been interpreted out of the Sherman Act, the Commission may gain control over agreements and abuses of dominant positions which so far have been the sole preserve of national authorities and law.

Negative clearance

Unlike Article 85, Article 86 does not provide for exemption, but an undertaking in a dominant position can apply for negative clearance under Article 2 of Regulation 17. This allows the Commission to certify that, on the basis of facts within its possession, there are no grounds for action on its part. It is, though, a statement of opinion, which may be altered should circumstances change. An undertaking which is doubtful whether some business practice or activity is in breach of Article 86, can notify the Commission, in the hope that it may receive negative clearance.

Negative clearance is thus a declaration of the Commission, subject to review, that it intends to take no action in respect of Article 86 (or 85). The granting of negative clearance can be rescinded should things change. Also it does not bind the national courts or the ECJ. It would therefore not prevent another undertaking, who complains of being adversely affected by a dominant firm, from seeking legal redress. Where full disclosure has been made to the Commission, it would certainly mitigate against any fines that may be imposed should the negative clearance be withdrawn.

Enforcement

There are three main ways in which Article 86 can be enforced. These are:

(1) by the Commission under the powers conferred on it by Regulation 17;
(2) by the national authorities under Article 88 of the Treaty;
(3) by legal action taken by undertakings or individuals who have been adversely affected by the abuse of a dominant position.

Enforcement by the Commission

The two main powers of the Commission in relation to dominant positions are an order to end the infringement under Article 3 and the imposition of fines and penalties under Article 15 of Regulation 17.

Article 3 states that:

Where the Commission upon application or upon its own initiative, finds that there is an infringement of Article 85 or Article 86 of the Treaty, it may by decision require the undertakings . . . concerned to bring such infringement to an end.

The Commission can thus act on its own initiative, or on a complaint by a third party. Those entitled to make application for an investigation by the Commission are Member States, and natural or legal persons who claim a legitimate interest.

The possibility of an abuse of a dominant position may come to the notice of the Commission in a number of ways. In the first place it keeps its 'eyes and ears' open. It makes studies of market structures, and under Article 12 of Regulation 17, it can institute a general enquiry into specified sectors of the economy. This it has done where the flow of trade between Members States appears to be distorted, or in some way other than it would be, if normal competitive forces were in operation. The result of these enquiries may discover the presence of a dominant undertaking who is acting in such a manner as to distort the market.

Secondly, matters may be notified to the Commission by the various agencies in the Member States, such as the Office of Fair Trading in the United Kingdom, or the Kartelamt in Germany. These authorities keep a close watch on the operation of market forces within their own countries.

The main source to the Commission of infringements of Article 86 are complaints by undertakings who allege they are being, or may be, damaged by a dominant position of another undertaking. Thus a firm may complain that it is being deprived of supplies, or being subjected to unfair prices or other trading conditions. The Commission investigation in *AKZO (1983)* was made following a complaint of discriminatory and predatory pricing by a competitor who alleged they were being priced out of the market. The Commission in fact encouraged such complaints, and has established a complaints procedure to make it easy to disclose possible infringements.

Whether to make an investigation on its own initiative, is within the discretion of the Commission. When a complaint is made formally to the Commission, however, it is under a duty to act, provided the complaint is admissible. A complaint must be more than mere denunciation, but must fulfill certain conditions, and allegations have to be substantiated in some material way. When an admissible complaint is made, but the request for action is dismissed by the Commission, this non-action is in the nature of a legal act, as well as any action it may take, and is thus subject to an appeal to the ECJ and judicial review.

Obtaining information

The Commission is given considerable power to obtain information by Regulation 17. Under Article 11, it is given the authority to request, national authorities and undertakings, to provide it with all the necessary information it may require. It is certain whether there is any duty to comply with the request, but if information is provided, it must not be false or misleading as otherwise penalties may be imposed. However, if an undertaking does not comply with a request, the Commission can make a decision requiring the undertaking to supply the information within a specified period of time, indicating the penalties for noncompliance. There is no power to make a decision against national authorities, such as the Office of Fair Trading.

Under Article 14, the Commission has the power to enter premises, inspect books and other business records, to take copies of records, and to ask for oral explanations. Undertakings are bound to submit to this sort of investigation provided it is ordered by a decision of the Commission. Penalties can be imposed on those undertakings which do not comply.

Fines and penalties

The Commission has the power to impose fines and penalties on undertakings who are in breach of Article 86, or who fail to comply with a Commission decision, subject to review by the ECJ.

Under Article 15, fines of from 1,000 to 1 million ECU, or 10 per cent of turnover, whichever is the greater, can be imposed on an undertaking for negligent or intentional breaches of the competition rules. Fines can also be imposed, ranging from 100 to 5,000 ECU for supplying false or misleading information, or for failing to comply with a Commission decision to supply information or open their books and records for inspection.

Under Article 16 the Commission can also impose periodic penalty payments of between 50 and 1,000 ECU per day to compel an undertaking to put an end to an infringement of Article 85 or 86 in accordance with a decision taken under Article 3 of the Regulations. Fines and penalties, like decisions, are legal acts and therefore subject to judicial review by the ECJ. Under Article 192, they are enforced by national authorities in accordance with national law procedures.

Enforcement by national authorities

National authorities are also, by virtue of Article 88 of the Treaty, competent to apply Articles 85 and 86. But by Article 9 of Regulation 17, they can only do so provided the Commission has not commenced proceedings. Although Article 88 was often used prior to the passing of Regulation 17, particularly by the Kartelamt in Germany, it is probable that the occasions when a national authority would take it on itself to enforce the competition rules will be very rare indeed. In fact the Office of Fair Trading has never used these powers.

Enforcement by individual action

As the Treaty, and Regulations issued under it, are intended to have direct effect in the Member States, then an individual who has suffered harm as a result of an infringement of Articles 85 and 86, can bring an action in the United Kingdom courts for redress for breach of statutory duty. In *Application des Gaz v Falks Veritas (1974)*, the Court of Appeal expressed the view that breaches of Article 86 constitute new heads of tort in English law, an opinion which was confirmed in *Garden Cottage Foods Ltd v Milk Marketing Board*.

In this case, GCF claimed damages and an injunction against the Board for a refusal to supply. The High Court awarded damages on the grounds that damages provided a sufficient remedy, but the Court of Appeal substituted an injunction. On Appeal to the House of Lords, the injunction was quashed on the technical ground that the Court of Appeal cannot substitute its own discretion for that of the judge at first instant.

The House, however, gave its clearest indication yet that a person who has suffered harm through a breach of Article 86 can claim damages and/or an injunction. Lord Diplock, with whom the majority agreed, stated that:

> As the prohibitions in Articles 85 and 86 tend by their very nature to produce direct effects in relations between individuals, these Articles create direct rights in respect of the individuals concerned, which the national courts must safeguard.

and that a breach of Article 86 is:

> A breach of a statutory duty that is imposed . . . for the benefit of private individuals to whom loss or damage is caused by a breach of that duty.

If the competition rules of the EEC are to be enforced at national level by the national courts, then it is important that use is made of Article 177 of the Treaty in order to ensure a uniform interpretation throughout the Common Market. Article 177 provides that where a point of Community law is raised before a national court, the court may, and if it is a final court of appeal, must refer the matter to the ECJ for an interpretation of the relevant law. In this way the ECJ can maintain control over the interpretation of Articles 85 and 86 in order to see that they are applied in a similar way in all Member States.

Conclusion

Recent cases brought under Article 86 have given rise to some concern. Korah (1975) has suggested that Article 86 is being used to protect smaller and medium-sized firms against the larger ones, and is therefore preventing the efficient firm from expanding at the expense of the inefficient. The interests of consumers and the economy as a whole, in the encouragement of efficiency, are being subordinated to the interests of the smaller businesses.

From the *United Brands* case, it seems as though that once an undertaking has a substantial share of the market, and is considerably larger than its competitors, then it may be treated as being in a dominant position, even though it is still facing competition. The case also suggests that the Commission and Court may be placing a too narrow definition of the market, thus a relatively small firm can be dominant if the market is defined in a particularly narrow way.

Once a finding of dominance has been reached, then it is difficult for an undertaking to discriminate, even if there can be positive public benefits from such discrimination. So in *Garden Cottage Foods Ltd. v Milk Marketing Board*, the rationalization of the marketing system of the Board, which led to the exclusion of the plaintiff company, along with several others, from obtaining further supplies of butter from the Board, was put at risk. Does this mean then that a dominant firm now cannot re-appraise its dealer network in order to provide a more efficient service to consumers? If a dominant firm dismissed one of its dealers, so refusing to supply in the future, then it faces the possibility of being fined by the Commission.

Perhaps the remedy lies in paying less attention to the anti-competitive effects of certain business practices which now fall within Article 86, and concentrating instead on the effects on the public interest. If a firm in a dominant position engages in some business practice which has positive benefits to consumers and the public in general, then that practice should not be condemned because it has some anti-competitive effect.

6

Merger Control

Introduction

There are a number of ways in which a dominant situation may arise. An undertaking may simply be more efficient than its competitors, thus gaining a larger share of the market. A dominant situation can also arise through the exercise of patent rights, the control of its suppliers or distributors, or having access to greater financial resources. There is little the law can do to prevent such situations arising, the concern of the law in these cases being to prevent the abuse of market power. But one of the most common ways in which a monopoly or dominant position can come about is through mergers, and it is through exercising control over mergers that the law can be effective in the control of market power. Merger control is aimed at preventing the monopoly or dominant situation from arising, rather than controlling the abuse of the situation once it has arisen.

Merger control is found in Part V of the Fair Trading Act, 1973. As in the case of monopoly control, the system of control used is one of reference to, and investigation by, the MMC though only the Secretary of State can make a merger reference. He does, however, have the advice of an advisory panel chaired by the Director. The EC Commission also has the power to control mergers under Article 86, where there is likely to be abuse of a dominant position which may affect trade between Member States.

Types of merger

There are two main ways in which mergers can be implemented. In the first place it can involve a transfer of shares, so that the shares in what were previously two independent undertakings, are now under the same ownership and control. Secondly, it can involve the transfer of assets from one undertaking to another, as distinct from a transfer of shares. The important thing is that what were once two separate enterprises are now brought under the same ownership or control.

Mergers can be classified in three different ways. First, mergers can be 'horizontal', that is, between two firms at the same stage in the chain of distribution, e.g. two manufacturers or two retailers who were previously in competition with each other. Secondly, a merger can be 'vertical', that is, between two firms at a different stage in the chain of distribution, e.g. a retailer takes over one of its suppliers (backward integration), or a manufacturer takes over a retailer (forward integration). Finally a merger can be 'diversified' or 'conglomerate'. This occurs where the parties to the merger are not in competition with each other, but carry on business in different fields, e.g. a tobacco company takes over a company which produces food. Not all mergers fall neatly into one of these classifications. Some may fall into more than one category, such as where a brewery, wishing to enter the tourist and leisure market takes over a chain of hotels. This is both diversified and vertical.

Most mergers are of the horizontal kind, the fewest being vertical mergers. In the 1982 Annual Report of the Director General of Fair Trading, it was stated that the Office of Fair Trading examined 190 mergers during the year. Of these, 65 per cent were horizontal, 30 per cent diversified, and 5 per cent vertical. Reports show that although the percentage of vertical mergers had remained fairly steady at 5 per cent, the number of horizontal mergers has fallen from 85 per cent in the period 1965–8, while diversified mergers have increased by some 20 per cent. Of these 190 mergers which were examined, ten were referred to the MMC, one against the advice of the Director.

Horizontal mergers have a direct effect on competition,

because, of course, there is a reduction in the number of independent firms operating in the market. However, competition need not necessarily be reduced. It may actually increase, the market becoming more competitive. So a merger may be effected between two or more small firms in order to be able to more effectively meet the competition of a dominant firm.

Vertical mergers also effect competition, though the effect is more indirect. Where a manufacturer takes over one of its suppliers, this can effect competition in two ways. The supplier may be required only to supply its parent company, and the parent may only obtain its supplies in the future from the new subsidiary. In a forward integration, the situation can be used to promote group products at the expense of those of its competitors.

The effect on competition of a diversified merger is not so clear. The greater financial resources of the undertaking created by the merger can, and often does, strengthen its position in the market. Further it may use its greater resources to undercut competitors in one market, its losses being made good from profits made in other markets. The enlarged group may also possess greater economic power in general, though not dominant in any one particular market, and this in itself may be objectionable (see Cunningham, 1974).

The effect on competition is not the sole, or even the most important criterion for controlling mergers. The main criteria is the effect on the public interest, of which the reduction in competition may be a part. Thus in the proposed merger between Charter Consolidated and Anderson Strathclyde (1982), the factors considered by the MMC as to why the merger may operate against the public interest, were the possible loss of management effectiveness, adverse effects on labour relations, and adverse effects on employment in Scotland. The secretary of state did not accept the report, and allowed the merger to go ahead.

Merger situation

Section 64 of the Fair Trading Act provides that a merger situation exists where it appears that two or more enterprises, one of them carried on in, or controlled from, the United Kingdom, have ceased to be distinct enterprises, and either:

(a) a monopoly situation relating to the supply of goods and services, supplied in the United Kingdom, or a substantial part of it, will be created or intensified; or
(b) the value of assets taken over exceeds £15 million.

Ceased to be distinct enterprises

Before the secretary of state can make a merger reference, the enterprises which are the subject of the merger must have ceased to be distinct. An enterprise is defined in section 63 (2) as the activities, or any part of the activities, of a business. Thus, if an undertaking sells part of its business to another business, this could be the subject of a merger reference.

Section 65 (1) provides that any two enterprises shall cease to be distinct if either:

(a) they are brought under common ownership or control; or
(b) either of the enterprises ceases to be carried on at all because of any arrangements entered into to prevent competition between the enterprises.

A very wide meaning is given to 'common control' by section 65 (2). This provides that enterprises shall be regarded as being under common control if they are:

(a) part of a group of companies, as defined by section 154 of the Companies Act, 1948;
(b) carried on by two or more companies of which the same person, or a group of people have control; or
(c) carried on by a company, and by a person or group of people who have control of that company.

Therefore, it can be seen that as well as the common, and more normal situation, where a company is part of a group, control also exists where one person controls two companies, or where one person runs a business, and then acquires a controlling influence in a company that carries on another.

Section 65 further provides that control exists where a person, without having a controlling influence is nevertheless able to materially influence the policy of a company, or is materially able to influence the policy of the person carrying on the enterprise. So, for example, a person who holds a controlling interest in one company, then becomes managing director of another, may be able to influence policy without holding shares of the latter company. It may be that if a person lends money to a company, say a merchant bank, then the bank may be able to influence policy. In both of these instances a merger situation may arise. In fact the definition of control is so wide that little attempt has been made by businessmen to avoid the provisions of the Act (see Korah, 1975).

Criteria for reference

Before a merger reference can be made, a monopoly situation must be created or intensified, or the value of the assets to be taken over must exceed £15 million. The monopoly situation, which is created or intensified is where one-quarter of goods and services supplied in the United Kingdom, or a substantial part of it, are supplied by, or to, the same person. Thus, the same market share used for a monopoly reference is used for a merger reference.

One difference between a monopoly and a merger reference is that, for a merger reference, the part of the United Kingdom must be a substantial part. In a monopoly reference the person making the reference can limit the reference to a part of the United Kingdom, and the MMC is bound by that limitation. Presumably, in a merger reference, the MMC could find that the reference does not comply with the Act, because the part of the United Kingdom is not a substantial part.

The second criterion for reference is that the value of the assets taken over exceed £15 million. This enables a reference to be made when market share is not affected, as in a diversified or vertical merger. One peculiarity of the asset value criterion is that when a reverse take-over is made, a reference may not be able to be made. Thus, if a firm with an asset value of £20 million took over a firm with an asset value of £12 million, no reference can be made unless the market share criterion is satisfied. If the position was reversed a reference could be made. Most merger references are made under the asset value criterion, and in fact, out of the ten references made in 1982, nine of them were made under this heading.

Section 64 requires that only one of the companies which is a party to the merger needs to carry on business or be controlled from the United Kingdom. This means that a merger reference can be made if a United Kingdom company takes over a foreign company, or more likely, a foreign company acquires control over a United Kingdom one. This therefore allows the secretary of state to exercise some form of control over the acquisition of United Kingdom companies by overseas companies. This was a major factor in the MMC concluding it would be against the public interest, for the Hongkong and Shanghai Bank, and the Standard Chartered Bank, to take over the Royal Bank of Scotland. The MMC concluded that the transfer of ultimate control of a significant part of the clearing bank system outside the United Kingdom would have an adverse effect, opening up possibilities of divergence of interest, and in particular, adverse effects on the Scottish economy. In a dissenting opinion, however, one member of the MMC did not accept that the proposed mergers would have such an adverse effect on Scotland sufficient to constitute a detriment to the public interest of the United Kingdom. The Secretary of State accepted the majority view, and asked the Director to obtain undertakings not to proceed with their proposals to acquire control. These undertakings were given.

Anticipatory mergers

Most of the provisions relating to merger control relate to mergers which have already taken place. The most effective way to control mergers though, is to prevent them happening. This power is given in section 75, which applies the other provisions relating to mergers, to proposed mergers. In practice, most merger references are brought under this section. The normal practice is to postpone a proposed merger pending the report on the reference. If the parties to the proposed merger refuse to agree to suspend action, the secretary of state can make an order under section 74, prohibiting them from proceeding with the merger.

The reference

Under section 76, the Director is required to take steps to keep himself informed about merger activity, but only the secretary of state can make a reference. He does, however, take advice on whether to make a reference from the mergers panel, which is chaired by the Director. This preliminary investigation by the mergers panel normally takes a maximum of 3 weeks, as it is undesirable to keep the parties to a merger in suspense as to whether a reference is to be made for any period of time.

The secretary of state must make the reference within 6 months of the time when the enterprises ceased to be distinct, though this period can be extended to 6 months after the date the secretary of state ought to have known of it. This generally poses few problems in practice because most references are of proposed, rather than completed, mergers.

As with monopoly references, the content of the reference will be precise. A merger reference cannot be restricted to the facts in contrast with a monopoly reference. Section 69 requires the MMC to investigate and report on two questions. These are:

(a) whether a merger situation qualifying for reference has been created; and
(b) if so, whether the creation of that situation operates, or may be expected to operate against the public interest.

All merger references are therefore public interest references.

The investigation

The MMC is under a statutory duty under section 5 (1) of investigating and reporting on any question referred to it regarding the creation, or possible creation, of a merger situation qualifying for investigation. Under section 72, the MMC must include in the report definite conclusions, the reasons for those conclusions, and a survey of the general position with regard to the subject matter of the reference.

If the MMC find that a merger situation qualifying for investigation has been created, and that the creation of that situation operates or may be expected to operate against the public interest, the MMC must specify in their report the particular effects which are adverse to the public interest. They must also consider what action shall be taken, and may make recommendations as to such action.

The criteria as to what may be contrary to the public interest are laid down in section 84 (7). These criteria are not exclusive, and the MMC is allowed to take into account any factor which they think would be against the public interest. This involves a calculation of costs and benefits. The effect on competition is an important factor, as is the possible adverse effects on efficiency. Other adverse factors which the MMC has taken into account include the effects on management, employment prospects, overseas control, possibility of higher prices and the effect on labour relations. On the other hand a merger can bring positive public benefits such as increased efficiency and the advantages of scale. Other beneficial factors have included the effect on the balance of payments, the injection of better management, competing more effectively with foreign competition, and improved research and development prospects. The MMC thus has to balance the possible adverse effects with the possible benefits. So in the proposed ICI/Arthur Holden (1982) merger the MMC thought there would be some distortion of the market, and lessening of competition in the home market. They concluded, however, that the benefits accruing from the merger, in particular a stronger industry able to compete more effectively with foreign competition outweighed the detriments.

Subsequent action

If the MMC reports that a merger situation qualifying for investigation does not exist, or if it does, the merger may not be expected to operate against the public interest, then that is the end of the matter. There is no power given to the secretary of state to prohibit a merger following a favourable report of the MMC. If the report is adverse, then this can lead to either informal or formal action.

There is no duty, however, on the secretary of state to follow the recommendations of the MMC if the report is adverse. He can still allow the merger to go ahead. Thus in the Charter Consolidated/Anderson Strathclyde merger reference, the MMC concluded that the proposed merger might operate against the public interest, and recommended, by a majority, that it should not go ahead. Nevertheless, the secretary of state allowed the merger to proceed.

Informal action

Under section 88, the secretary of state can require the Director to consult with the relevant parties in order to obtain from them appropriate undertakings, that they will not take any steps to proceed with the merger. The Director must keep such undertakings under review. If the parties refuse to give an appropriate undertaking, then the Director will advise the secretary of state who may then exercise the order making powers under the Act.

Formal action

The order making powers available to the secretary of state, set out in Schedule 8 of the Act, have already been discussed in relation to monopoly control. The powers are very wide, and include divestment or demerger. However, as most references are anticipatory, the normal order will be one to prohibit the merger, or only to allow it subject to certain conditions. As most parties to a proposed merger are prepared to give appropriate undertakings, it is very rarely that an order needs to be made.

Newspaper mergers

Separate provisions are made in relation to newspaper mergers. Briefly, the provisions are that it is illegal to transfer a newspaper to the owner of other newspapers, without the prior consent of the secretary of state. Section 58 (1) states that the transfer of a newspaper, or its assets, to a newspaper proprietor whose papers have a circulation per day of 500,000 or more copies, together with that of the newspaper transferred shall be unlawful and void without the written consent of the secretary of state. This consent can only be given after reference of the proposed merger to the MMC unless the secretary of state is satisfied that the paper to be transferred is not economic as a separate paper, and that it is not intended to continue publication, or the average circulation of the paper transferred is less than 25,000 copies per day.

When a newspaper reference is made the MMC must report on the public interest aspects, which must include regard to the need for accurate presentation of news and free expression of opinion.

Mergers under Article 86

The Treaty of Rome contains no Article that deals with mergers. However, it is clear from the *Continental Can* case that if one firm in a dominant position takes over another firm, this may be an abuse of a dominant position. Continental Can concerned a US multinational which had acquired control over a German firm producing metal containers. The German subsidiary took over a Dutch metal can producer, the control of both the German and Dutch companies being invested in one holding company, created and controlled by Continental Can. The EC Commission saw the acquisition of the Dutch company as being a breach of Article 86. They argued that the German company was in a dominant position, and that, therefore, the acquisition of the Dutch company meant that they would no longer compete against each other.

Although the ECJ did not agree that Continental Can were in a dominant position, it did support the view of the Commission that Article 86 could be used to control mergers, saying that:

> . . . Article 86 is . . . also aimed at (practices) which are detrimental through their impact on an effective competition structure such as mentioned in Article 3 (f) of the Treaty. Abuse may therefore occur if an undertaking in a dominant position strengthens such position in such a way that the degree of dominance reached substantially fetters competition.

Article 86 is a very imperfect instrument of merger control, because it only applies once a dominant situation exists. This means that if two or more undertakings, none of whom are individually in a dominant position, decide to merge, then the Commission cannot take any steps until the merger is complete. It cannot prevent the merger. If an undertaking which is already in a dominant position attempts to take over another firm, and this strengthens its competitive position, then the Commission could presumably step in, as this could be the abuse of a dominant position. In fact, since Continental Can, the Commission has not attempted to use its powers to control mergers, except under the Coal and Steel Treaty which does give specific powers of merger control in those industries.

The Commission has proposed a Regulation to the Council, which would provide the Commission with the power to exercise control in respect of all types of mergers, whether horizontal, vertical, or diversified. The Regulation would also require certain proposed mergers to be notified to the Commission. So far the Council has not been able to come to any agreement on the Regulation, and the position is one of great controversy.

Conclusion

The net effect of a merger depends upon the balance between the potential benefits (scale economies, spreading risk, improved managerial performance following take-over, 'synergy' between two management teams) and the costs in terms of economic and managerial efficiency which may follow if substantial monopoly power is acquired. This balance will vary from case to case, but both policy and the law seem to exhibit a general presumption in favour of mergers. Very few mergers are prevented. Between 1977 and 1981, the Office of Fair Trading reviewed 1,019 proposed mergers, and of these, only twenty-seven were referred to the MMC. In nine of these cases, the reference was set aside because the parties concerned decided not to proceed with the merger. In fact it is not uncommon when a firm makes a take-over bid for the offer to be conditional on the proposed merger not being referred to the MMC. Of the remaining eighteen references the MMC reported adversely in only eight, and of these the secretary of state allowed one merger to proceed, and in two other cases, the merger was allowed to proceed subject to certain undertakings being given. Over a period of 5 years, then, only five proposed mergers were prevented.

This relatively lenient approach to mergers is consistent with the 'competitive' view of the economy, in which the merger process is seen as one of the major ways in which resources are channelled into the more efficient organizations. On the other hand, there has been increasing scepticism about the benefits of scale economies and 'synergy', and it could be argued that the general presumption in favour is going rather too far.

In the *Review of Monopolies and Mergers Policy* (Leisner, 1978), it was proposed that the law should adopt a more neutral rather than favourable approach. It suggested that the MMC should be required to specify whether the merger would prevent, restrict, or distort competition, and also to specify any other adverse effects. Then the report should contain any benefits which the merger would bring about. The adverse effects should then be balanced against the likely benefits, and the report should recommend what action should be taken. It did not, however, propose that the MMC should find against a merger, unless it considers that the merger is in the public interest. Until this is done the legal control over mergers is likely to remain weak.

7

Restrictive Trading Agreements

Introduction

It has been seen that the legal control and regulation of monopoly is not very strong, or at least, the powers that exist are not rigorously enforced. A much stronger line is taken against restrictive trading agreements, though, as we shall see, the sanctions against non-registration are rather weak. This area of control is almost entirely concerned with behavioural factors, structural features being of much less importance. Structural factors may, however, be relevant in deciding whether a particular agreement passes through one of the 'gateways', or in influencing the Director in whether or not to ask the secretary of state for a direction not to refer to the Court.

The control over restrictive agreements, apart from where a monopoly situation existed first came into effect with the Restrictive Practices Act 1956, since amended and extended, and the current law is contained in the 1976 Act. The Act requires certain types of restrictive agreements or arrangements to be registered with the Office of Fair Trading. Once registered the Director is under a duty, with some exceptions, to refer the agreement to the Restrictive Practices Court. If the Court find the agreement contrary to the public interest, then the agreement is void and it is unlawful to give effect to it. The burden of proof is on the parties to the agreement to show that it is in the public interest, but they do not have an entirely free hand. They must satisfy the Court that one of the statutory defences applies, the so-called 'gateways', and the agreement must be capable of passing through one of these gateways. There is the further requirement that even, if this is satisfied, it must be shown that on balance, the agreement is not contrary to the public interest.

It is traditional to divide restrictive agreements into two categories – vertical and horizontal. Vertical agreements are those between firms at different stages of production, that is, between buyer and seller of goods or services. The most common types of vertical agreement are:

(1) sole distributor agreements, where a manufacturer gives the sole right to a distributor or dealer to sell his products within a particular area, in return, usually, for a promise from the distributor or dealer not to sell the product outside his area, or to sell the product of a competing manufacturer;

(2) the tying-in agreements whereby a manufacturer will only sell a particular product to a dealer on condition that the dealer agrees to purchase other products from the manufacturer's range;

(3) the resale price maintenance agreement whereby the manufacturer lays down the price at which the goods must be retailed.

Horizontal agreements are those between competitors who are at the same stage of distribution. They directly restrain trade, unlike vertical agreements which have an indirect effect. The more common type of horizontal agreements are:

(1) price fixing agreements;
(2) market sharing agreements;
(3) agreements to restrict output;
(4) agreements to maintain resale prices by collective action; and
(5) collective boycotts of those who do not comply with certain restrictions.

In the main, the Restrictive Practices Act is concerned with horizontal rather than vertical agreements, because, as will be seen later, the Act exempts from registration some of the more common types of vertical agreement, such as exclusive dealing and resale price maintenance. Resale price maintenance agreements are now subject to separate legislation, while exclusive dealing agreements may be caught by the Competition Act as anti-competitive practices.

Agreements requiring registration

When the Restrictive Practices Act was first passed in 1956, the only agreements called up for registration were restrictive agreements in relation to goods. Since then, the 1968 Act gave the Secretary of State the power to call up for registration information agreements relating to goods, and the Fair Trading Act added restrictive and information agreements relating to services. The current law is now contained in the 1976 Restrictive Practices Act. There are, therefore, four types of agreement which are liable to registration. These are:

(1) restrictive agreements relating to goods;
(2) restrictive agreements relating to services;
(3) information agreements relating to goods; and
(4) information agreements relating to services.

Restrictive agreements relating to goods

Restrictive agreements relating to goods which require registration are defined in section 6 of the 1976 Act. This section provides that:

This Act applies to agreements (whenever made) between two or more persons carrying on business within the United Kingdom in the production or supply of goods, or in the application to goods of any process of manufacture, whether with or without other parties, being agreements under which restrictions are accepted by two or more parties in respect of any of the following matters—

(*a*) the prices to be charged, quoted or paid for goods

supplied, offered or acquired, or for the application of any process of manufacture to goods;

(b) the prices to be recommended or suggested as the prices to be charged or quoted in respect of the resale of the goods supplied;

(c) the terms or conditions on or subject to which goods are to be supplied or acquired or any such process to be applied to goods;

(d) the quantities or descriptions of goods to be produced, supplied or acquired;

(e) the process of manufacture to be applied to any goods, or the quantities or descriptions of goods to which any such process is to be applied; or

(f) the persons or classes of persons to, for or from whom, or the areas or places in or from which, goods are to be supplied or acquired, or any such process applied.

To be registrable an agreement must be 'between two or more persons carrying on a business within the United Kingdom', and the agreements must be one 'under which restrictions are accepted by two or more parties'. The first requirement is, therefore, that there must be an agreement between two or more persons. As the Act treats companies who are members of the same group as one company, an agreement between a parent company and any of its subsidiaries, or between any two or more subsidiaries of the same parent company would not be registrable as it would not be an agreement between two persons.

Secondly, the two or more persons who are party to the agreement must be carrying on business within the United Kingdom. An agreement between a United Kingdom company and a foreign company, which did not carry on a business in the United Kingdom whereby they agreed not to export to each other's countries, a market sharing agreement which would otherwise come within section 6, is not registrable, even though the agreement restricts imports of goods, and so weakens the competition faced by the United Kingdom company. Of course, the United Kingdom company could face a monopoly reference, if it was in a monopoly situation, or a competition reference under the

Competition Act. The agreement may also be void under Article 85 of the Treaty of Rome if the agreement affects inter-community trade.

Finally, two or more parties to the agreement must accept restrictions. An agreement whereby one party only accepts restrictions is not registrable. Suppose two firms, A and B, make an agreement whereby A agrees not to sell his products in a particular part of the country in competition with B. B pays A for his promise but is under no restrictions himself. As restrictions are imposed only on one party to the agreement, then the agreement is not registrable, even though this type of agreement restricts competition in a part of the country just as much as a market sharing agreement where both parties are under restrictions.

The persons who accept the restrictions need not be carrying on business in the United Kingdom. If two English firms, A and B, make an agreement with two foreign firms, C and D, whereby the two foreign firms agree not to sell their products in the United Kingdom this is a registrable agreement, even if no restrictions are accepted by the two English firms. The English firms satisfy the requirement as to two or more persons carrying on business in the United Kingdom, while the two foreign firms satisfy the latter requirement.

Trade associations

Section 8 extends the registration requirements to agreements or recommendations made by trade associations, a trade association is a body of persons formed for the purpose of furthering the trade interests of its members.

Section 8 (1) provides that an agreement made by a trade association shall be treated as though the agreement were made by all the members of the association. If a manufacturer makes an agreement with a trade association that he will only supply his product to the members of the association in return for an agreement to give preference to that manufacturer's product then this agreement is registrable.

But the Act goes further than this and applies to trade association recommendations, even if the members of the association are not bound to follow those terms. Section 8 (2) and (3) states that where recommendations are made by a trade association as to the action to be taken or not to be taken in respect of the matters described in section 6 (1), the Act has effect as if the agreement contained a term that each member agrees to comply with those recommendations. For the purposes of registration, recommendations made by an association are treated as binding even though members are free to ignore them if they so wish. A trade association recommendation that members should only deal with specified persons, or should raise their prices by fixed amounts would, therefore, be registrable.

Exemptions from registration

Certain agreements which would otherwise be registrable are exempted from registration by section 9 and Schedule 3 of the Act. Section 9 contains a number of restrictions which can be disregarded in deciding whether or not the agreement is registrable. Exempted agreements under section 9 include those restricting competition between producers and distributors of coal and steel (sole competence in this area is conferred on the European Commission by Article 65 of the ECSC Treaty); restrictions relating to employment; and restrictions relating to the application of the standards of the British Standard Institution.

Of more general application is the exemption in section 9 (3). This provides that in deciding whether or not a restrictive agreement is registrable, no account shall be taken of any term which relates exclusively to the goods supplied. The most important class of agreement which at one time was exempted from registration was the individual resale price maintenance agreement. These are now subject to the control of the Resale Prices Act, 1976. The type of restriction which may be disregarded is one whereby the dealer agrees not to sell goods supplied to him outside a particular area, provided that agreement is between one seller and one buyer, and not part of some wider agreement or arrangement.

Section 9 states that the restrictions can be disregarded for the purpose of registration. If, therefore, an agreement contains other restrictions the agreement will be registrable. However, if A and B entered into an agreement which imposed restrictions on each other, and the restrictions on A were to be disregarded, there is now only one person who has accepted restrictions. The agreement would, therefore, not be registrable as two or more persons have not accepted restrictions under it. Assume that A is a supplier of components to B, and this is a substantial part of A's business. B contemplates setting up his own factory to manufacture these components, but A offers to continue to supply B at a special low price, in order to keep B's business in return for B not setting up his own factory or purchasing components from elsewhere. Here A has restricted himself as to the price he will continue to supply B, and B has restricted himself in two ways – not to establish his own factory and not to buy from elsewhere. The restriction on A, as to the price to be charged is to be disregarded as relating exclusively to the goods supplied, so the agreement is not registrable as the only restrictions left are accepted by one person.

Under Schedule 3 will be found a collection of agreements which do not require registration. It includes agreements expressly authorized by statute; certain agreements relating to patents and trade marks; where all the restrictions apply to exports; and to exclusive dealing agreements.

Exclusive dealing agreements are of particular interest and require further comment. Schedule 3, paragraph 2, provides that an agreement which only restricts the supplier from selling goods of a particular description to others, and the distributor from selling similar goods does not require registration. Thus, if A agrees to make B a sole distributor of his goods within a particular area in return for B promising not to sell goods of another supplier, then this agreement is free from registration. Sole distributor agreements are free from registration under the Act.

Restricting agreements relating to services

The power to call up for registration agreements relating to services was first included in the Fair Trading Act 1973, and is now contained in section 11 of the 1976 Act. The power was implemented by the Restrictive Practices (Services) Order, 1976. Section 11 provides that:

(1) The Secretary of State may by statutory instrument make an order in respect of a class of services described in the order (in this Act referred to as "services brought under control by the order") and direct by the order that this Act shall apply to agreements (whenever made) which—

    (a) are agreements between two or more persons carrying on business within the United Kingdom in the supply of services brought under control by the order, . . . ; and

    (b) are agreements under which restrictions, in respect of matters specified in the order . . . are accepted by two or more parties.

(2) The matters which may be specified in such order . . . are any of the following—

    (a) the charges to be made, quoted or paid for designated services supplied, offered or obtained;

    (b) the terms or conditions on or subject to which designated services are to be supplied or obtained;

    (c) the extent (if any) to which, or the scale (if any) on which, designated services are to be made available, supplied or obtained;

    (d) the form or manner in which designated services are to be made available, supplied or obtained;

    (e) the persons or classes or persons for whom or from whom, or the areas or places in or from which, designated services are to be made available or supplied or are to be obtained.

To a large extent the framework of control laid down is similar to that for the supply of goods. The agreement must be between two or more persons carrying on a business in the United Kingdom in respect of the supply of services brought under control, and two or more persons must accept restrictions in respect of the designated services. Arrangements, as well as agreements are covered, as are recommendations from service trade associations.

A distinction has to be drawn between 'controlled' services and 'designated' services. Controlled services are those which the parties to the agreement provide, while designated services are those to which restrictions apply. In the majority of cases the two will be the same. Thus, if a number of removal firms enter a price agreement, the restrictions relate to the service provided. If, however, the agreement also included the amount they would pay for insurance, the restriction does not relate to the service provided (Cunningham, 1974).

The Order calling up services for registration brough under control the whole range of services, both professional and commercial, which are capable of being provided. The Order also designated all services in respect of which restrictions are accepted, except for those which cannot be designated. These are listed in Schedule 1 of the Act and in the main include those services which are already regulated by professional associations, and include the services provided by lawyers, doctors, dentists, architects, professional engineers and accountants.

Exemptions from registration

Similar exemptions which apply to the registration of agreements relating to goods apply to services, with suitable modifications. Thus section 18 (2) states that no account shall be taken of any restriction which relates exclusively to the services supplied, and of any term relating to standards approved by the British Standards Institution. Schedule 3 allows complete exemption from agreements relating to exports, patents and exclusive dealing with regard to services as well as goods. Thus, an agreement between a building society and an estate agent whereby the estate agent agreed not to act as agent for any other building society in return for the building society not using any other agent within a certain area is not registrable.

Information agreements

Information agreements are those whereby the parties agree to exchange information on certain matters such as prices, costs of production, quantities produced, stocks, etc. These agreements were not subject for registration under the 1956 Act, yet in certain cases they can have the same effect as if there were a restrictive trading agreement. As a result the 1968 Act, now section 7 of the 1976 Act, gave powers to the Secretary of State to call up for registration information agreements relating to goods on a number of topics such as the prices, terms of supply, quantities produced, costs, persons to whom supplied and the areas to which supplied.

One Order has been made so far, the Restrictive Trade Practices (Information Agreement) Order 1969, which calls for the registration of information agreements relating to the prices charged or to be charged for goods. Exchange of information agreements relating to prices are now on a par with other restrictive agreements, and similar rules apply. So there must be an agreement between two or more people carrying on business in the United Kingdom by which two or more agree to supply each other with information. The same exemptions from registration apply to information agreements. So, for example, if the information relates exclusively to the goods supplied, the restriction can be ignored. Also Schedule 3 exempts from registration agreements between a buyer and seller where the buyer agrees to supply information regarding the sale of other goods of the same description, and the seller to give information about sales to other persons of similar goods.

The Secretary of State also has the power to call up for registration certain exchange of information agreements relating to services, but so far no Order has yet been made.

Agreement and arrangement

The Act makes registrable both agreements and arrangements. Thus, the legislation extends over formal cartels at one end of the spectrum, to informal arrangements at the other. There is no need for an intention to be legally bound.

Section 43 provides that agreement includes any agreement or arrangement whether or not it is intended to be legally enforceable. The Act, however, contains no definition of the word 'arrangement', and reference must therefore be made to court decisions in order to attempt to discover how loose an arrangement has to be before it is outside the terms of reference.

One of the earlier cases in which the question of whether there was an arrangement was raised was the *Austin Motor Co. Ltd.'s Agreement (1975)*. Before the Act came into force, Austin had a marketing system based on multilateral contracts with distributors, dealers and retailers. The contracts contained various restrictions including restrictions as to the prices at which the retailers would resell; restrictions as to the persons to whom the distributors and dealers were permitted to sell; and restrictions as to from whom trade buyers could acquire cars. After the Act, the contracts would have been registrable, so Austin entered into bilateral contracts with each of its distributors or dealers separately. The agreements were carefully worded so that it would be exempted from registration under section 8 (3) of the 1956 Act, now section 9 (3) of the 1976 Act.

Austin sought a declaration from the High Court that the agreements were not registrable, and the Registrar (now the Director) conceded that taken separately each agreement was exempt from registration. The Registrar argued, however, taken together, the agreements constituted an arrangement, as none of the distributors and dealers would accept such restrictions unless he was satisfied that all other distributors and dealers were also bound. In effect the Registrar was arguing that the position in fact, if not in law, was no different than it was under the multilateral agreements. The courts rejected this argument, holding that for an arrangement to exist there must be some acceptance of mutual rights and obligations, even if these are not enforceable at law.

This case was followed by *British Basic Slag Ltd.'s Application (1962)*. Basic slag is a by-product of smelting used as a fertilizer. A number of steel manufacturers formed a company, British Basic Slag Ltd., each of whom owned shares in it and each appointing a director to the Board. Each manufacturer then entered into an agreement with British Basic Slag Ltd., whereby each agreed to sell all its slag to the company. Each agreement was bilateral, as in the Austin case, but each manufacturer was aware that other manufacturers entered into similar agreements, and relied on this knowledge when entering into it. Each individual agreement was exempt from registration, but the question for the court was whether there was a horizontal arrangement under which all manufacturers agreed not to sell any slag except to the Basic Slag company.

The court decided that there was an arrangement which was registrable. A wide definition of arrangement was given, Cross J. saying:

> . . . all that is required to constitute an arrangement . . . is that the parties to it shall have communicated with one another in some way, and that as a result of the communication each has intentionally aroused in the other an expectation that he will act in a certain way.

The manufacturers appealed, but the decision, and the definition of arrangement was confirmed, as was the definition of an arrangement given in the Austin case. Willmer LJ. pointed out that there was no inconsistency with the Austin case, where it was held that the parties did not accept mutual rights and obligations. In this case these were present, for he said:

> when each of two or more parties intentionally arouses in the other an expectation that he will act in a certain way, it seems to me that he incurs a moral obligation to do so. An arrangement as so defined is, therefore, something whereby the parties to it accept mutual rights and obligations.

For an arrangement to exist it seems that there must be some form of communication between the parties, and that by this communication, each arouses in each of the others an expectation that he will act in a particular way. Communication does not necessarily have to be by words, but can be inferred from conduct. In the *Conference Group of the Tyre*

Manufacturers' Conference Agreement (1966) certain firms expressly agreed to inform each other about the level at which bids had been made to firms hiring tyres to fleet operators, but the machinery established was also used to inform each other of the price he proposed to quote. Any party could, if he wished, revise his own quotation once he knew of others. As operated, the permissive part of the scheme meant that no party would quote a rate lower than the lowest rate notified without first giving notification of that lower quotation. It was accepted by the Court that each party decided independently to operate the scheme, and there was no verbal communication of these intentions. But the Court, once it became apparent that all parties operated the scheme, held there were mutual obligations to continue the scheme in return for the benefits extracted from it. The conduct of the parties in operating the scheme was sufficient to make this an arrangement.

The decision in the *Tyre Mileage* case means then, that mutual inter-communication is not essential to the creation of an arrangement. The conduct of the parties amounted to a representation as to future conduct, as none of the parties would have continued to notify his rates in advance if the others had not done so.

Cunningham (1974) points out that this observed conduct principle could lead to absurd situations. Assume, he says, that A announces a price increase, and sends a copy of his proposed increase to B, who then raises his prices to match A's. If this happens frequently, can the observed conduct of B in raising his prices to match A's constitute an arrangement? At no stage is B obliged to raise his prices, and A's action in putting up his prices is not dependent on B following suit. Korah (1976) also gives a similar example. If firms normally follow the price increases announced by any one of them, though there is no agreement to do so, it could be argued, she says, that each has aroused expectations that it is likely to follow any change. It is probable that price leadership does not amount to an arrangement unless firms communicate with each other in words or conduct, before publishing a price change, and in doing so they have led each other to expect certain action and done something to encourage the others to rely on it occurring.

It is apparent that the definition of an arrangement is vague and uncertain, and in fact it is possible that firms could enter into arrangements without being aware of the fact. This could have serious consequences, particularly if the arrangement is one which involves the breach of an undertaking not to enter into a registrable agreement. As Cunningham (1974) points out, the business community is entitled to some clear definition of what constitutes a registrable agreement and arrangement.

Reference to the Court

Once an agreement has been registered, it is the duty of the Director to refer the agreement to the Restrictive Practices Court. Before referring the agreement to the Court, however, the Director may try to persuade the parties to the agreement to withdraw the restrictions, or end the agreement, thus avoiding the need for reference.

Although the Director has a duty to refer to the Court any agreement which he thinks contain restrictions which he cannot get removed by agreement, he will consider the possibility of making an application to the secretary of state for a direction discharging him from his duty to refer. Under section 21 (2), the Director can ask the secretary of state for a direction not to refer an agreement in cases where the restrictions are not of such significance as to require an investigation by the Court.

In deciding whether to make a representation under section 21 (2), the Director examines each case, which is treated on its merits. Agreements which involve price fixing or collusive tendering are rarely regarded as suitable for a representation, and these are usually referred even if all the restrictions are abandoned after registration. In fact any restriction which appears capable of causing detriments, either to the general public or to other traders, is treated in principle as a matter of significance. It is then up to the parties concerned whether they wish to abandon the agreement, remove the restriction, or defend it before the Court. It is important to note that it is the restrictions which must be insignificant and not the agreement in itself. A significant agreement in which all

the restrictions are insignificant is suitable for representations.

In the 1980 Report of the Director General of Fair
Trading, there are illustrated several types of agreement
which have often met the criteria for the Director seeking a
direction not to refer. For instance, the recommendation of
standard terms and conditions for the supply of goods or
services is a common practice, and these recommendations
would require registration and referral to the Court in the
normal course of events. Standard terms are often very
desirable, not only in the interests of the supplier, but also of
the consumer. They are not necessarily regarded by the
Directors as having a significant effect on competition, but
the terms must be fair and reasonable, not misleading, and
not contain clauses void under the Unfair Contract Terms
Act (1977). The benefit to customers of standard terms must
outweigh the detriment to them of being unable to negotiate
more favourable ones, and in general, standard terms must
be variable to meet special circumstances.

The 'Gateways'

If the Director cannot persuade the parties to remove
restriction from the agreement, or he feels that he cannot
make a request for a direction under section 21 (2), then the
agreement is referred to the Court for a decision as to
whether the agreement should be declared void. The Act
provides that the parties can bring forward defences, but it
does not allow them a free hand. Those who wish to defend
an agreement will have to satisfy the Court that one of the
eight criteria laid down in section 10 (section 19 in the case
of services) have been satisfied, that is that the agreement
passes through one of the 'gateways'.

The criteria laid down in section 10 (section 19 uses similar
words in relation to services) are:

(a) that the restriction is reasonably necessary to protect the
public from injury;
(b) that the removal of the restriction would deny to the
public as users, purchasers or consumers, substantial
benefits;

(c) that the restriction is reasonably necessary to counteract measures taken by a person who is not a party to the agreement;

(d) that the restriction is reasonably necessary to enable those who are party to the agreement to negotiate fair terms for the supply of goods (or services) to or from a person who is in a dominant position;

(e) that the removal of the restriction would have a serious effect on the level of employment;

(f) that the removal of the restriction would cause a reduction of exports;

(g) that the restriction is necessary to support another restriction which is not against the public interest; or

(h) that the restriction does not directly or indirectly restrict competition to any material degree.

The task faced by parties to an agreement in steering it through one of the 'gateways' is a difficult one. Even if they succeed in this, the problem of the 'balancing tailpiece' has to be overcome. Sections 10 and 19 provide that the Court must be further satisfied that the restriction is not unreasonable having regard to the balance between the benefits of the agreement and any detriment to persons not parties to the agreement or to the public.

The difficulty can be illustrated by reference to one of the first cases to come before the Court, the *Yarn Spinners' Agreement (1959)*. An association of cotton spinners entered into a price fixing agreement in order to protect themselves in a contracting industry. Without the agreement the spinners feared cut-throat competition which would result in many firms ceasing to trade with the consequent loss of jobs. The association attempted to get the agreement validated by the Court by steering it through gateways 'b' and 'e'. With regard to gateway 'b', that the public would be denied substantial benefits if the restrictions were removed, the association argued that:

(1) the agreement provided price stability which was of benefit to the public, particularly during recessions of which many were foreseen. Further the price of yarn had only a minimal effect on the prices of finished products;

(2) the price controls enabled the maintenance of a reserve capacity during recessions so that advantage could be taken of any upturn when it came;

(3) as the spinners could not compete in price, they had a greater incentive to compete in other ways, such as improving the quality or giving better service; and

(4) since many firms would go out of business, there was the possibility of the emergence of a monopoly situation as mergers and rationalization took place.

These arguments failed to convince the Court. The agreement kept prices higher than they would otherwise have been, and the price stability was only obtained at the expense of a free market. The Court thought that price stability as an alternative to a free market does not, as a general rule, confer a benefit to the public, and in any case it was contrary to the general presumption embodied in the Act that price restrictions were contrary to the public interest.

The Courts were equally unconvinced of the argument that the agreement helped to maintain spare capacity, as in a declining industry it was desirable that capacity should be reduced, so that a more compact industry would emerge. By keeping high costs firms in business the agreement contributed to inefficiency, which impeded the industry's export performance. With regard to the two other arguments the Court thought there was no evidence in favour of the agreement. The benefit of competing in other ways was negligible and the possibility of a monopoly emerging was not considered a serious possibility.

The agreement did however pass through gateway 'e'. The association was able to show to the satisfaction of the Court that there would be a serious adverse effect on employment if the restrictions were removed and that the effect would be persistent. The Court thus had to bring the balancing tailpiece into operation, and they held that although the consequent unemployment effects would be serious, the detriments arising from the absence of competition more than outweighed the forecast unemployment. The agreement was thus declared void by the Court.

As this agreement was a key arrangement in a major industry it attracted much attention and criticism. If this agreement could not pass the scrutiny of the Court, the prospects for others were bleak, and in fact the decision was followed by the abandonment of many agreements on the register. Great emphasis was placed by the Court on free competition which was regarded as essential to the public interest. Both price stability and rising unemployment were considered as of less benefit than the free market, and the case was an important landmark to a more competitive economy.

Gateway 'a' – protection against injury

Only three cases have been reported of attempts to pass through this gateway, and all have failed. In fact, few restrictions will pass this test as where there is a risk of injury, regulations are normally made by the government. This gateway was pleaded in the first case to come before the Court, *Chemist's Federation Agreement No. 2 (1958)*, which concerned restrictions designed to ensure that proprietary medicines were only sold in shops where there was a qualified pharmacist, in order to reduce the risk of harm through self medication. It was held that the risk of injury was not sufficiently great to warrant the restriction, and that the restriction in any case would not afford adequate protection.

The other two cases were the *Tyre Trade Register Agreement (1963)*, and the *Motor Vehicle Distribution Scheme (1961)*. In the former case the tyre manufacturers were to grant terms only to dealers who complied with certain standards, including the presence of a qualified fitter. It was argued that the restrictions were necessary to prevent accidents from incorrect fitting of tyres. The argument was rejected by the Court on the grounds that there was no guarantee that the qualified fitter would actually do the fitting, and that incorrect tyres was not a major factor in road accidents. The latter case required the manufacturers to prescribe the retail prices of their products and the discounts which would be allowed to registered dealers. These were dealers who met certain requirements regarding the qualifications of staff and space. The Court was not satisfied that the scheme did anything to protect the public from injury.

Gateway 'b' — substantial public benefits

This is by far the most popular gateway because of its broad character. It has been seen, however, from the *Yarn Spinners* case, that it is by no means easy to pass through. The criterion to be applied is that of a substantial benefit to the public as purchasers, consumers, or users of goods, or as users of services. It is not enough to show that there is no detriment to the public, or that the agreement is fair and reasonable. It must be shown that there are positive benefits to the public.

It has been seen from the *Yarn Spinners* case that price stability is not considered by the Court to be a benefit to the public. In *Scottish Association of Master Bakers' Agreement (1959)* the Court confirmed the view taken in the *Yarn Spinners* case, and stated that it is only stabilization at the right prices that benefits the public, and that as a general rule price stabilization is not a satisfactory alternative to a free market. The argument that a price war leads to a lowering of quality is another argument that has not been accepted by the Court in a number of cases. In *Linoleum Manufacturer's Agreement (1961)*, the argument that to terminate the price agreement would lead manufacturers to introduce a new cheaper grade of linoleum and thus a lowering of quality was not accepted. On the contrary, the Court thought that this would improve consumer choice provided that the old qualities were still made available.

Where the parties have been able to show that the restrictions have kept prices down, the agreements have been allowed to stand as benefiting the public. So in *Cement Maker's Federation Agreement (1961)*, the price fixing scheme attracted new capital to the industry, and the return on capital was, as a result, 5 per cent less than it had been in a free market. This resulted in substantially lower prices. And in the *Net Book Agreement, 1957 (1962)*, the argument that termination of the agreement would lead to smaller orders for printing and binding, and thus to higher prices, was accepted.

Another argument that has been accepted is that of saving firms the trouble of 'going shopping'. In *Black Nut and Bolt Associations Agreements (1960)*, the association, which comprised some forty-four members supplying over 3,000 standard items, in addition to non-standard ones, operated a price ring. Although vital to industry, the products of the association represented only a minute portion of the value of the finished product. Without the fixed prices, the buyers would have had to make a great many inquiries of various manufacturers before placing an order. This would have increased transaction costs, which would have been very high in relation to the cost of the product. The agreement, therefore, had benefits which outweighed the lack of competition. This argument has not however been successful in other cases where it has been raised. But in *Black Nut and Bolt*, speed of delivery was essential, the cost of the product was very low in relation to the finished product and in relation to transaction costs, and the products came in a large number of shapes and sizes. These features were not present in the other cases defended under this head.

Other arguments that have been accepted include avoiding a reduction in the number of outlets, avoiding a reduction of stocks to unsatisfactory levels and promoting technical co-operation.

Gateway 'c' – countering anti-competitive measures

An agreement will pass through this gateway if it can be shown that the restrictions are necessary to counteract measures taken by a person outside the agreement to prevent or restrict competition in the business in which the parties to the agreement are engaged. The gateway has not yet been considered by the Court, but presumably it refers to the situation where on the same side of the market there is a dominant firm who is engaging in anti-competitive practices, and a number of smaller firms who enter into a restrictive agreement in order to counteract the dominant position.

The gateway refers to one person, which could be a group of companies, so it would not apply if a number of firms entered into a cartel in order to counteract another cartel. If this was allowed it would be possible for an industry to consist of two cartels, each necessary to counter the power of the other. The gateway does not refer to the size of the 'person', but unless that person is of sufficient dominance to affect the market, he would not be able to enter into anti-competitive practices which would harm others. No reference is made to the public interest, so this point would be raised when looking at the balancing tailpiece.

Gateway 'd' – counteracting a dominant buyer or seller

This enables a number of small firms on one side of the market to enter a cartel to counteract the dominant position of a person on the other. So if there is a dominant seller, and a number of buyers enter into a purchasing agreement to negotiate terms with the seller, the purchasing restrictions may pass through this gateway. As in the previous gateway, the dominant buyer or seller must be a single person, so one cartel cannot be used to counteract the power of another cartel. This also extends to cartels formed to counteract the power of a foreign cartel, even though that cartel would not be subject to registration.

Only one case has so far passed through the gateway, the *National Sulphuric Acid Association's Agreement (1963)*. Here, United Kingdom manufacturers formed a joint purchasing pool to negotiate with a dominant seller in the United States, who supplied about 50 per cent of sulphur sold in the United Kingdom. The restrictions required the parties to the agreement to pay a common price and not to acquire sulphur otherwise than through the pool. The US company was held to be in a dominant position and the restrictions passed through the gateway. On the other hand in *Wire Ropes Agreement (1965)*, the National Coal Board, who purchased 38 per cent of the United Kingdom sales of wire rope were held not to be a dominant buyer. In fact, the NCB bought over 90 per cent of one kind of wire rope but the Court held that this was not a separate market from other wire ropes.

Gateway 'e' – preserving employment

A restriction in an agreement may be upheld if it can be shown that to end the restriction would have a serious and persistent adverse affect on employment in an area or areas in which the industry is concentrated. The gateway is probably, therefore, only available in those industries which are heavily concentrated in certain areas of the country, such as cotton. In fact, *Yarn Spinners* is the only case which passed through the gateway, although it failed the balancing tailpiece.

It is probable that this gateway will rarely be of use, as it would be difficult to show that maintaining high prices would also maintain employment. There is a strong argument that to maintain inefficient, high cost producers in business by a price cartel will inhibit investment in the more efficient firms, as they will lack the incentive to invest. This lack of investment in the long run could lose more jobs than those saved by the cartel.

Gateway 'f' – maintaining exports

If the removal of the restrictions is likely to cause a substantial reduction in exports, then they may pass through this gateway. The reduction in exports can be either of volume or value, and may relate to all exports, or to exports of a particular industry. The latter alternative is important because a small reduction in the exports of a major exporting industry may have a substantial effect on the balance of payments, while a large reduction in exports of a minor industry may have very minor overall effect.

It appears that this gateway was included in order to help the balance of payments, yet it applies only to a reduction in exports. If the removal of restrictions would lead to a substantial increase in imports this would not enable it to pass through the gateway. In the *Linoleum Manufacturer's Agreement (1961)*, it was held that import payments should not be deducted from export receipts in order to assess the effect on exports if the restrictions were terminated. This gateway has frequently been argued, but it has only been passed in one case, *Watertube Boilermakers' Agreement (1961)*. Here the agreement required the members to meet whenever an enquiry was received. At this meeting, information was exchanged, and a member selected. After selection the quotations were tabled and only the selected member could lower his price to the lowest price quoted. The main object was to obtain the order for the United Kingdom, and as over 40 per cent of output was exported, the Court was satisfied that if the restrictions were removed, the number of foreign orders might be reduced.

Gateway 'g' – ancillary restrictions

This covers restrictions reasonably necessary to support other restrictions upheld by the Court. For example, in *Black Nut and Bolt*, where the price cartel passed through gateway 'b', the agreement also contained restrictions as to standard terms and conditions of sale. These restrictions were upheld by the Court under this gateway. Obviously, a restriction cannot be upheld unless another restriction has already passed through one of the previous gateways. It therefore applies only to subsidiary restrictions.

Gateway 'h' – no material effect on competition

This gateway was added by the 1968 Act, and requires little explanation. It has only been used once, in *Scottish Daily Newspaper Society's Agreement (1972)*, where the printers of daily newspapers in Scotland agreed not to publish whilst a strike at one of their members was continuing. It was upheld because the restriction was only temporary and therefore not material in restraining competition. It will in fact only be rarely that this gateway will be pleaded, as in cases where the restrictions are immaterial, the Director will normally exercise his discretion under section 21 and ask the secretary of state for a direction not to refer to the Court. The addition of the gateway, however, has probably encouraged the Director to seek directions in more cases.

Balancing tailpiece

Even though a restriction has passed one of the gateways, the agreement must still satisfy the balancing tailpiece to section 10 or section 19. This provides that the restriction is not unreasonable having regard to the balance between the benefits of the restriction, and any detriments to the public or persons not party to the agreement. Thus in the *Yarn Spinners* case, although the agreement passed through gateway 'e' as it helped to preserve employment, these benefits were outweighed by the detriments to the public in having to pay higher prices. On the other hand in the *Boilermakers* case, the detriments to the purchasers of boilers in having to pay higher prices did not outweigh the export benefits, while in the *Blanket Manufacturer's Agreement (1959)*, the benefits of minimum quality outweighed the detriments of the lack of cheaper blankets. The Court, it would appear, faces a difficult task in weighing up benefits and detriments, and, as Cunningham (1974) says, is this the sort of economic argument which the Courts should be engaged in?

Enforcement

Failure to register

If an agreement which is subject to registration under the Act is not registered, then, under section 35, the agreement is void in respect of the restrictions or information provisions, and it is unlawful to give effect to, or enforce the agreement in respect of the restrictions or information provisions. Thus, if a party to an unregistered agreement failed to keep to the agreement, then no action could be brought for breach of contract. If attempts were made to enforce the agreement by, say, withholding supplies of goods or refusing to supply services, then those attempts would be unlawful.

Section 35 (2), though, makes it clear that no criminal proceedings lie against a person who gives effect to, or attempts to enforce a non-registered agreement. However, a person who has suffered loss as a result of the operation of restrictions in an unregistered agreement can sue for damages for breach of statutory duty. For example, a person who has had his supply of goods cut off, or a person who has been a victim of collusive tendering, and thus paid a higher price, can recover damages. Civil actions are, however, rarely brought because of the difficulties of establishing a claim. The plaintiff must show that there was an unregistered agreement, that effect was given to it, and that he is directly affected by the failure to register. Further, he must also show that he has suffered loss and the amount of that loss. A person who has been the victim of collusive tendering may have difficulty in establishing what a competitive price would have been.

The most effective sanction is the power of the Court to make an Order under section 35 (3). This provides that on the application of the Director, the Court may make such Order as the Court thinks fit, to restrain any party to the agreement from giving effect to or enforcing

(a)   the agreement in question in respect of any restrictions or information provisions; and
(b)   any other unregistered agreement.

Breach of the Order would be contempt of Court, punishable by fines or imprisonment.

The consequences can be very serious for persons subject to such an Order. It is possible for registrable agreements to be made unknowingly, because the implications are not realized, and as agreement also includes arrangement and that there is no clear definition of what constitutes an arrangement, it can be seen that great care would have to be taken by those subject to an Order. In fact, very few Orders have been sought by the Director and his predecessor, the Registrar. The Director will only seek an Order in those cases where he is not satisfied that the unlawful acts would not recur. An Order under section 35 (3) (then section 7 (3) of the 1968 Act) was made in the *Flushing Cistern Maker's Agreement (1973)*, where a price ring had operated unregistered for several years. The Court stated:

. . . that agreements have been operated for years in disregard of the provisions of the Act by responsible company officers in a position to discover the law, who have throughout had a duty to comply with the law. . . . This constitutes a grave and persistent dereliction of the duty of responsible company officers so to direct and manage the company affairs as to comply with the restrictive practices legislation. . . . In the view of this Court, an injunction is required to bring home to all these companies that their standards in respect of this legislation have not been high enough. . . .

This case does illustrate one of the main weaknesses of the sanctions which are available to enforce the legislation. A restrictive agreement can have operated for years, and yet there is no power to impose a fine. The only sanctions that are available relate to the future, that is to restrain the parties to the agreement from giving effect to or enforcing the agreement. There is no way of penalizing firms for persistent and prolonged breach of the law, except to issue an order which relates to future conduct. There is nothing equivalent to the situation in the USA, where it is a criminal offence, or in West Germany, where the Kartelamt has the power to impose fines for breaches of their restrictive practices legislation, though under EEC legislation the Commission has the power to impose fines and penalties.

Restrictions against the public interest

The reason for the reference to the Court by the Director of a registered agreement is to obtain a declaration from the Court as to whether the restrictions or information provisions are, or are not, in the public interest. Section 2 (1) provides that where any restrictions or information provisions are found by the Court to be contrary to the public interest, then the agreement shall be void in respect of those restrictions or information provisions. Further, under section 2 (2) the Court may on the Director's application, make such Order as appears to be proper to restrain the parties to the agreement from giving effect to, or enforcing the restrictions or information provisions, and from making any other agreement to like effect.

The Court can only make an order on the application of the Director, and it is the policy of the Director not to apply for an order unless he is not satisfied that the parties will abide by the declaration. But the Court has the discretion whether to make an order or not. In practice the Court will normally accept an undertaking from the parties concerned, rather than issue an injunction, unless there are circumstances where the Court is not satisfied with the conduct of the parties and feels an injunction will be more appropriate. There is, however, no major difference between an injunction and an undertaking as far as the sanctions for breach are concerned, as in both cases, breach is a contempt of court.

As well as preventing the parties from operating the condemned restrictions, the order can also prevent the parties entering into an agreement to the like effect. This is necessary, as otherwise the parties could circumvent the law by terminating the original agreement, and making another one. The Director brought contempt proceedings in the *British Concrete Pipes Association's Agreement (1981)*, against four companies for allegedly breaking an undertaking given to the Court in 1965 that they would not enter into, or make any other agreement to the like effect as an agreement between members of the British Concrete Pipe Association in respect of restrictions declared to be contrary to the public interest. The companies were parties to agreements registered in 1979, and it was held that, as these agreements were of like effect to those in respect of which undertakings had been given, the parties were in contempt of Court and fines of up to £100,000 were imposed.

Conclusion

The United Kingdom legislation on the control of restrictive practices is 'form based', rather than 'effects based' as is the case in the European Community and in many other countries. As was stated in the Review of Restrictive Trade Practices Policy (1979):

> The control of restrictive practices in the United Kingdom applies only to agreements which contain restrictions of a form specified by law. By contrast the Treaty of Rome and the legislations of a number of countries control those agreements or arrangements which have the purpose or effect of restricting competition.

Agreements or arrangements have to be registered only if they comply with the requirements of the Restrictive

Practices Act, and those agreements which do not come under the Act, even if they have the effect of restricting or preventing competition do not have to be registered. Conversely, even if agreements do not have any effect on competition, they must still be registered, though in these cases the Director can seek directions not to refer, and if he does not seek such directions, the agreement may pass through gateway 'h'. It would appear desirable to introduce an effects based system by including a requirement that agreements or arrangements must have the effect of restricting, preventing or distorting competition, though the Green Paper rejected the proposal on balance. They preferred the present system to be retained, but adapted to overcome some of the weaknesses. Some step in this direction has been made, however, in the Competition Act, by enabling the Director to investigate and if necessary refer to the Monopolies Commission, non-registrable agreements and practices which adversely affect competition.

Two main defects in the current legislation appear to be present, apart from the form based system. In the first place, the chances of steering restrictions through one of the gateways is extremely difficult, and the legal form here is probably too strict. Successfully steering a restriction through one of the gateways except for the last one involves proof of something positively advantageous, and even then the balancing tailpiece has to be satisfied. It can also be questioned whether a legal process is a satisfactory method of resolving economic questions as to whether an agreement is in the public interest. The *Yarn Spinners* case illustrates the balancing act the Court has to apply. Here the Court had to decide whether the public interest was better served by higher unemployment and lower prices, of lower unemployment and higher prices. In the event the Court decided in favour of the free market, and, thus, the former alternative. A court of law is probably not the place where such decisions should be made.

On the other hand, the means of enforcement is rather weak and should be strengthened. Combined together, the strictness of the Court's interpretation of the public interest, together with the lack of any effective sanction on the failure to register, means that there is a disincentive to register restrictive agreements. Thus, in the Monopoly Commission's investigation into the supply of flour and bread, seventy-seven unregistered agreements relating to bread discounts were uncovered. There seems a strong case for imposing a penalty for non-registration of agreements which come under the Act, and for making it a criminal offence to engage in certain types of anti-competitive activity such as collusive tendering. The Director should also have the power to approve certain agreements without the necessity of either seeking a direction not to refer, or of referring them to the Court.

8

Restrictive Agreements in the EEC

Introduction

Collusive activity between undertakings, as well as being subject to national law, is also subject to the competition rules of the EEC. The EEC Treaty provides for the establishment of a system in order to prevent the restriction or distortion of competition in the Common Market. If businessmen were allowed to enter into private arrangements which erected barriers to trade between Member States, then the implementation of a common market would be frustrated. Trade barriers created by undertakings in a dominant position were considered in Chapter 4. Competition can equally be distorted by collusion between undertakings. As the first Commissioner responsible for competition policy stated:

> . . . it would be useless to bring down trade barriers between Member States if . . . private industry were to remain free . . . through cartel-like restrictions on competition, virtually to undo the opening of the markets. (European Parliamentary Assembly Debates, 1961)

It is to prevent 'cartel-like' restrictions that Article 85 is included in the Treaty. Whereas Article 86 is aimed at the abuse of a dominant position, Article 85 is aimed at preventing various types of collusive activity which have an adverse effect on competition within the Common Market. It differs from the registration requirements of the Restrictive Trade Practices Act in that it is framed in very general terms, and catches all forms of collusion which have an effect on competition in the Common Market.

Unlike the procedure under the Restrictive Trade Practices Act, there are no registration requirements, but a system of notification has been established. Notification to the Commission is essential if exemption or negative clearance is claimed. Also, in contrast to the powers under the Restrictive Trade Practices Act, the Commission can impose substantial fines and penalties on those undertakings which are in breach of Article 85, and not merely prohibit similar activities in the future.

Prohibited agreements

Article 85 (1) provides that:

> The following shall be prohibited as incompatible with the Common Market; all agreements between undertakings, decisions by associations of undertakings, and concerted practices which may affect trade between Member States, and which have as their object or effect the prevention, restriction or distortion of competition within the Common Market, and in particular those which:
>
> (a) directly or indirectly fix purchase or selling prices or any other trading conditions;
> (b) limit or control production, markets, technical development, or investment;
> (c) share markets or sources of supply;
> (d) apply dissimilar conditions to equivalent transactions with other trading parties, thereby placing them at a competitive disadvantage;
> (e) make the conclusion of contracts subject to acceptance by the other parties of supplementary obligations which, by their nature, or according to commercial usage, have no connection with the subject of such contracts.

The various practices which are included in Article 85 (1) are not intended to be exclusive, but illustrative, in contrast with the position under the Restrictive Practices Act, where the restrictions must be in respect of the matters included in the Act. Any activities or practices carried on by undertakings are therefore caught by Article 85 (1), provided they come within the stated conditions. These are:

(1) there must be some form of collusion between undertakings;
(2) trade between Member States must be affected; and
(3) there must be some adverse effect on competition within the Common Market.

Collusion between undertakings

Article 85 requires some form of collusion between undertakings, otherwise it has no application, though Article 86 may be relevant. This collusion can take the form of an agreement, a concerted practice, or a trade association decision or recommendation.

The Treaty does not define an undertaking, but it must have legal standing under the Treaty. This generally means that the undertaking must have a legal personality of its own, and therefore includes any natural or legal person. It also appears from the decision in *Prym/Beka (1973)* that a partnership, even though it does not have a legal personality of its own, will be treated as an undertaking for the purpose of Article 85.

The Commission and the ECJ have treated companies within a group as a single undertaking, even though each company has its own separate legal personality. Competition law tends to look behind the veil of incorporation, and take account of the economic realities. A company which is controlled by another company does not have economic independence from its parent. Therefore companies within a group are not in competition with each other, and an agreement between associated companies would not be a breach of Article 85 (1), as it would not be an agreement between undertakings. The Commission, in *Christiana and Nielsen (1969)*, held that the sharing of markets within a group of companies is merely an allocation of tasks within a single unit, a view confirmed by the ECJ in *Centrafarm v Stirling Drug Inc. (1974)*.

The term undertaking must therefore be viewed in the broadest sense, covering any entity, from small, individually run businesses, to large, multinational companies, which are engaged in economic or commercial activities, including professional services.

Agreements These include not only contracts which are legally binding, but also informal 'gentleman's agreements', which are not intended to be legally enforceable. This was made clear in the *Quinine Cartel (1969)*, where a number of undertakings entered into agreements fixing prices and quotas world wide, except for the Common Market. When the agreements were extended to the Common Market by a non legally binding agreement, it was held to fall within Article 85 (1).

Concerted practice Even where there is no form of agreement at all, parallelism of behaviour can have an effect on competition. This is why collusion in the form of a concerted practice is included in the Article. A concerted practice was defined in *ICI v EC Commission* (Dyestuffs case 1969) by the ECJ to be:

A form of co-operation between undertakings which without having reached the stage where an agreement has been concluded, knowingly substitutes practical co-operation between them for the risks of competition.

In this case the behaviour of producers of dyestuffs in the Common Market was such as to lead the ECJ to believe that they were not actively competing against each other on the matter of price, though there was no evidence of any agreement, either formal or informal. On several occasions identical price increases were announced within days of each other. These price increases also varied in different parts of the Common Market, depending on what the market could bear. This behaviour pointed to collusion and was thus a concerted practice.

Parellelism of behaviour is not always identified with a concerted practice. Where there is a market leader, it is commercial prudence to follow the market, and similar conditions would apply in an oligopoly situation. Uniformity of price will also manifest itself in perfect competition. This was recognized in Dyestuffs by the ECJ. It stated that parallelism of behaviour is not in itself evidence of collusion, but is nevertheless likely to constitute a strong indication of a concerted practice if it leads to conditions in the market which do not equate with normal market forces. This is especially so, as in Dyestuffs, where the behaviour leads to price equilibrium at a different level from that which would have resulted from competition. A concerted practice can thus be said to be any form of co-operation between undertakings which reduces the risks of competition, and which affects normal market conditions.

An illustration of behaviour which was held to be a concerted practice occurred in *Hasselblad (G. B.) Ltd. v EC Commission (1984)*. Here, the exclusive dealer of a product in a Member State was faced with competition from a former authorized dealer. The sole distributor made test purchases from the dealer to determine the origin of the products, and then requested distributors in other Member States not to supply the former dealer.

Decisions of associations   Members of trade or professional associations are often bound by the rules of the association, which may cover such things as prices, quotas, the persons with whom they can deal, and terms and conditions of contracts. These can have a material effect on competition, thus distorting the market, and are caught by Article 85 (1). But the Article goes further than this, and includes trade association recommendations, even though these are merely guidelines, and there is no obligation on members to comply. Thus in *Vereeniging van Cementhandelaren v EC Commission (1973)* a trade association recommended the prices at which members should sell their products. It was held by the ECJ, confirming the decision of the Commission, that even though the recommended prices were not binding on members, they nevertheless allowed the members of the association to foresee with reasonable accuracy, what the behaviour of competitors was likely to be. This therefore distorted competition.

Affect trade between Member States

Any agreement must effect trade between Member States, and this is given the same interpretation as under Article 86. Any agreement which has an effect on the competitive structure of the Common Market will be treated as affecting trade between Member States, even though the movement of goods between Member States is not apparently or directly affected. But agreements which have no effect on trade at all, for example in relation to warning labels on dangerous products, or where agreements have an impact within one Member State only, or only outside the EEC, will not be caught by Article 85 (1).

However the fact that all the parties to an agreement are located in one Member State, or even outside the EEC, will affect interstate trade if the effect of the agreement is to isolate a national market. The ECJ has gone further than this, as has been seen in such cases as *Commercial Solvents* and *VCH*, discussed in Chapter 4, and have held that any agreements covering the whole of the territory of a Member State will be treated as affecting trade between Member States, thus almost interpreting this condition out of the competition rules.

The effect on trade must be significant. So in *Volk v Vervaecke (1969)*, a German producer gave the sole rights of sale in Belgium and Luxembourg to a Belgian distributor. The ECJ held that as the producer's share of the market in Germany was only 0.2 per cent, the effect on trade was insignificant, and said that:

To be capable of affecting trade between Member States, the agreement must . . . permit a reasonable expectation that it could exercise an influence on trade trends between Member States in a direction which would harm the attainment of the objectives of a single market.

Effects on competition

The object or the effect of the agreement must be to prevent, restrict, or distort competition within the Common Market. Article 85 (1) then goes on to include a number of prohibited activities. These, as has been noted, are merely illustrative, and it is open to the Commission to attack any form of activity which has the object or effect of adversely affecting competition.

A distinction must be made between 'object' and 'effect'. If the object of the agreement or practice is to restrain competition, it is irrelevant whether in fact it has that effect. In *WEA-Filipacchi Music (1973)*, a French record company made an agreement with its resale agents that they would not export to Germany. This was done to protect German distributors. As the market price in Germany was some 50 per cent higher than in France, the French sales agents wished to be free from the restriction in order to sell on the more lucrative German market. The Commission ordered the deletion of the export ban, dismissing the argument that the agreement had little, if any, effect on competition, WEA controlling only a minor part of the record market. The object of the agreement was to restrict competition, and this was sufficient to be caught by Article 85 (1). There was no need to make a market analysis to establish what effects the agreement had on competition within the Common Market.

Where an agreement does not have the object of restraining competition, it is still caught if it has the effect, in practice, of doing so. In this case a market analysis is necessary in order to discover the effects on competition, particularly for practices not listed in Article 85 (1). In *Société Technique Minière v Machinenbau Ulm (1966)* the ECJ laid down that where the agreement does not have as its object the distortion of competition, then:

> . . . the consequences of the agreement should then be considered and for it to be caught by the prohibition it is then necessary to find those factors which show that competition has in fact been prevented, restricted or distorted to an appreciable extent.

The effect on competition, like the effect on trade, must be appreciable or significant. Though the effect of an agreement may not be significant in itself, the cumulative effect of several similar agreements can have a significant or appreciable effect on competition, and thus fall within Article 85 (1). In *Brasserie de Haecht v Wilkin & Wilkin (1968)*, for instance, a Belgian cafe owner agreed to sell only beers and other drinks supplied by a particular brewery, a typical tied house arrangement. When sued for breach of contract, he successfully contended that the agreement was void under Article 85 (1). The ECJ stated that a contract cannot be isolated from its economic context, and though the agreement in itself had an insignificant effect on competition, the fact that other cafe owners had entered into similar agreements was considered highly relevant. A whole series of identical agreements can, in total, have a materially adverse effect on competition, even though each agreement taken itself has no such effect.

It has been argued that Article 85 only applies to horizontal agreements, vertical agreements coming within Article 86, provided that one of the parties is in a dominant position. This argument holds that Article 85 is only concerned to prohibit agreements that prevent, restrict, or distort competition between the parties to the agreement. Vertical agreements, such as exclusive distributor arrangements, do not restrain competition between the parties, but between one of the parties and outsiders. It is clear that Article 85 applies both to horizontal and vertical agreements. In *Consten and Grundig v EC Commission (1966)*, which involved a vertical exclusive distributor agreement, the ECJ stated that:

> Article 85 refers in a general way to all agreements which distort competition within the Common Market and does not lay down any distinction between those agreements based on whether they are made between competitors operating at the same level in the economic process or between non-competing persons operating at different levels.

Article 85 (1), therefore, catches all agreements, whether horizontal or vertical, which have as an object or effect, an appreciable distortion of competition within the Common Market, and which have a significant effect on trade between Member States.

Nullity

If an agreement falls within Article 85 (1), it is, by Article 85 (2), 'absolutely void'. This means that the agreement is unenforceable by a national court if one of the parties to the agreement is being sued for its breach. It also appears from cases such as *Application de Gaz Falks Veritas (1974)*, and *Garden Cottage Foods Ltd. v Milk Marketing Board (1983)* that an infringement of Article 85 (1) constitutes a breach of statutory duty, and therefore creates liability to those harmed (see Chapter 5). The Bundesgerichthof in West Germany has also held that those injured because of a breach of Article 85 (1) can claim compensation.

One major problem faced by national courts asked to enforce an agreement concerns those notified to the Commission in order to claim exemption under Article 85 (3). The difficulty arises from the fact that only the Commission can grant exemption from Article 85 (1). National courts must apply Article 85 (2), and declare a contract void, even though the Commission may, at a later date, exempt the agreement. National courts can, however, suspend proceedings pending the decision of the Commission, but only if the Commission has itself started proceedings under Regulation 17.

At one time it was thought that agreements notified to the Commission had provisional validity until the Commission ruled otherwise. In *Portelange v Smith Corona (1969)*, the ECJ ruled that:

> The agreements envisaged by Article 85 (1) of the Treaty which have been duly notified . . . are fully valid as long as the Commission has not issued a decision pursuant to Article 85 (3).

Concern was expressed that the effect of provisional validity was reducing the impact of Article 85 in prohibiting anti-competitive practices, particularly in view of the time normally taken by the Commission to come to a decision. In fact, in many cases, the Commission does not reach a decision at all, but issues an administrative or 'comfort' letter informing parties that it sees no reason to take any action under the competition rules. These letters are not legal decisions of the Commission, and therefore have no binding effect, but are useful for guidance.

The ECJ reviewed the question of provisional validity in *Brasserie de Haecht v Wilkin & Wilkin (No. 2) (1973)* ruling that provisional validity only applied to old agreements, and that new agreements are not provisionally valid. Old agreements are those entered into before Regulation 17 took effect, and, probably, agreements in existence in New Member States at the time of accession, and notified within 6 months of accession.

Although there are sound economic reasons for denying provisional validity to agreements, there is nevertheless a risk involved for undertakings, who having notified the Commission of an agreement and are awaiting their decision, carry out their agreement, as a national court would have to declare it void. One answer to the problem is that national courts should be allowed to grant exemptions as well as the Commission (Kon, 1982). The main objection appears to be that it would lead to disintegration of competition policy in the Common Market, because of the lack of uniform interpretation of Article 85 (3) by the courts in different Member States. It could also be argued that the courts are not the ideal forums to make decisions on what is essentially an economic problem.

Korah (1975) argued that the national courts should treat agreements covered by 'comfort' letters as being outside Article 85 (1), otherwise:

> there is a danger that many agreements that increase competition, for instance by providing for joint research and development of a new product . . . may not be enforceable. Doubts about the validity of such restraints may inhibit the investment necessary to important collaborative venture.

Nullity is the only sanction provided by the Treaty itself for infringing Article 85. Regulation 17, however, gives the Commission considerable powers to enforce the competition rules. These are similar to those given in respect of Article 86, considered in Chapter 4. Thus the Commission can order the parties to terminate the probitied agreement, or impose a fine of up to 1 million ECU or 10 per cent of turnover, whichever is the greater. It can also impose penalties for carrying on the prohibited practice, after being ordered to put an end to it, of between 50 and 1,000 ECU.

Exemption

An important exception has been provided to the general rule that restrictive practices which affect trade between Member States are prohibited. Article 85 (1) can be declared inapplicable by the Commission if the restrictions in the agreement are sufficiently counterbalanced by a number of benefits. Article 85 (3) provides that any agreement, decision, or concerted practice −

which contributes to improving the production or distribution of goods or to promoting technical or economic progress, while allowing consumer a fair share of the resulting benefits, and which does not:

(a) impose on the undertakings concerned restrictions which are not indispensable to the attainment of these objectives;

(b) afford such undertakings the possibility of eliminating competition in respect of a substantial part of the products in question,

can be exempted from Article 85 (1).

Only the Commission is allowed to grant exemption, in order to maintain a uniformity of approach within the Member States. This is provided for by Article 9 of Regulation 17, which states that the Commission, subject to review by the ECJ, shall have the sole power to declare Article 85 (1) inapplicable. National courts, if required to rule on the validity of an agreement, cannot grant exemption.

All four of the conditions laid down in Article 85 (3) must be satisfied before an exemption can be considered. These conditions are cumulative and not alternative. In the first place there must be some clear objective advantages involved, such as improved research facilities, improved distribution, cost reductions, or increased productive capacity. Secondly, consumers must benefit in some way from these advantages, for example, by lower prices, improvement in quality, or wider choice on the market. Consumers do not merely mean the final users of the products, but also trade purchasers.

The final two conditions which must be satisfied are negative ones. The agreement must not contain restrictions which are not indispensable in order to achieve the beneficial results, and competition between the undertakings must not be substantially affected. Any attempt by the parties to isolate national markets, and prohibit parallel imports will never obtain exemption.

Where all the requirements are met, an exemption can be given, either on an individual basis, or by way of a group or 'bloc' exemption.

Individual exemption

If the parties to an agreement want to claim exemption from Article 85 (1), they must notify their agreement to the Commission. A system of notification was established by Articles 4 and 5 of Regulation 17, the former referring to 'new' agreements, the latter to 'old'. Notification must be made in writing on the official form issued by the Commission, called 'Form A/B'. The information submitted must be truthful and accurate, as the Commission can impose a fine of up to 5,000 ECU where incorrect or misleading information is supplied intentionally or negligently.

Although there is no duty to notify under the competition rules, the possibility of exemption, and negative clearance, is a strong incentive to notification. There are, however, certain agreements listed in Article 4 of Regulation 17 which are dispensed from notification. These are:

(1)   agreements between parties located in one Member State, and which do not relate to imports or exports, that is agreements which are purely local;
(2)   two party agreements in which the only restriction relates to prices and other terms of resale, or relates to the exercise of industrial property rights;

(3) agreements relating to the development of uniform application of standard or types, joint research and development agreements, and specialization agreements where market share is less than 15 per cent and turnover is less than 200 million ECU.

This dispensation from notification does not mean that the agreements are exempt, but merely that the Commission can grant exemption, or negative clearance even without notification. It is still open for the Commission to impose a fine or order termination of the infringement, or for a national court to declare an agreement void. In *Brasserie de Haecht v Wilkin & Wilkin (No. 2) (1973)*, the ECJ stated that dispensation from notification does not give protection to the agreement, but is merely an indication of the types of agreement or practices which are likely to merit exemption.

In the main, the agreements that need not be notified are those which are thought to do the least harm to competition and market integration, and are intended to limit the number of notifications. If the parties are in any doubt as to whether an agreement falls within one of the categories for which notification is not required, they should notify, otherwise exemption may not be possible.

A second reason for notification is that under Article 15 (5) of Regulation 17, the Commission cannot impose any fines for activities which take place after notification, and before the Commission comes to a decision. As the Commission often issues a 'comfort' letter, rather than take a decision, the parties can carry on with their arrangements secure in the knowledge that they cannot be penalized by the Commission. This benefit of immunity from fines only applies to notified agreements, and agreements covered by 'bloc' exemptions.

'Bloc' exemptions

In order to reduce the number of individual notifications of agreements seeking exemption, the Commission has been given the power to issue a number of 'bloc' or group exemptions with respect to certain categories of agreement. Any agreement, decision, or concerted practice which falls within the scope of a 'bloc' exemption need not be notified to the Commission. It is therefore a valid agreement, and can be enforced by the national courts, which are bound by the Regulations issued by the Commission in respect of such exemptions.

Regulations have been passed giving 'bloc' exemption for exclusive distributor and exclusive purchasing agreements, and specialization agreements. 'Bloc' exemptions are also proposed for selective distribution agreements in the automobile sector, patent licensing agreements and research and development agreements. 'Bloc' exemptions, provided the parties keep within the boundaries of the exemption provide legal certainty, and undertakings can be assured that their agreements will not be declared void, nor are they liable to be fined. These 'bloc' exemptions will be dealt with in more detail later in the chapter.

Negative clearance

Negative clearance, which has been considered in relation to Article 86, can also be given in relation to Article 85. It is a procedure enabling the parties to an agreement to obtain a declaration of the Commission, that on the basis of facts in its possession, their activities do not come within the scope of the competition rules. Unlike an exemption, which is a legally binding decision of the Commission, negative clearance is a mere statement of opinion. It is thus not binding on the national courts, nor on the Commission itself. National courts are, however, likely to give very serious consideration to a declaration of negative clearance, and it can be pleaded in mitigation in respect of any fines which may later be imposed by the Commission. Although the Commission can reconsider the granting of negative clearance, there have been no cases so far in which the Commission has gone back on a decision to grant negative clearance.

Negative clearance differs from an exemption, apart from the fact that it is not legally binding, in that it is a decision of the Commission that the agreement does not fall within Article 85 (1). Where the Commission grant an exemption, the decision is that the agreement is caught, but there are grounds for exempting it. As with exemption, negative clearance cannot be given unless the agreement is notified to the Commission. The Commission has, however, issued a number of Notices specifying that certain activities are outside Article 85 (1), thereby providing what are in effect 'bloc' negative clearances. Notices have been made relating to minor agreements, exclusive agency contracts, co-operation between enterprises and patent licensing agreements.

Agreements of minor importance

Many agreements, particularly those entered into by small and medium sized firms, will be covered by the Notice Concerning Agreements of Minor Importance (1970). Agreements covered by the Notice will not be considered to violate the competition rules because the economic effect is not significant enough.

The Notice indicates that, normally, agreements will not be caught by Article 85 (1) where the market share of the products which are the subject of the agreement, or competing or substitute products produced by the parties, is not more than 5 per cent of the market for such products within a substantial part of the Common Market, and the aggregate turnover of the parties does not exceed 50 million ECU.

Exclusive agency contracts

The Notice on exclusive dealing contracts with commercial agents (1962) announces that a contract made with an agent, who contracts business on behalf of a principal, does not infringe Article 85(1). The agent will only be considered a 'commercial agent', within the meaning of the Notice, if he does not bear any responsibility for the financial risks involved. It is limited to instances where the agent is integrated into the sales organization of the principal. In particular, a dealer will be deemed to be an independent trader, and not a commercial agent, where he holds stocks as his own property, he provides customer service at his own expense, and where he determines prices and other terms of business. In these circumstances the 'bloc' negative clearance will not apply.

Co-operation agreements

The Notice concerning agreements in the field of co-operation between enterprises (1968) indicates that the Commission welcomes co-operation between enterprises 'where such co-operation enables them to work more rationally and increase their productivity and competitiveness on a larger market.' The Notice lists some eighteen different forms of co-operation, which are deemed not to restrict competition.

Subcontracting

A subcontracting agreement is one where the subcontractor supplies goods or services on behalf of the main contractor in accordance with the main contractor's specifications. In the Notice concerning subcontracting (1978), the Commission has indicated that such agreements are not, of themselves, caught by Article 85 (1). However, the agreement must not prevent the subcontractor from meeting orders from other customers, and must not reserve solely for the contractor, the benefits of the subcontractor's research and development. The agreement can impose a restriction that the subcontractor can only use equipment and technology provided by the contractor for the purposes of the agreement.

Patent Licensing Agreements

In the Notice on patent licensing agreements (1962), the Commission considers that certain clauses in patent licensing agreements are unobjectionable in relation to Article 85 (1). These include:

(a) undertakings by the licensor not to grant other licences, or exploit the invention himself;
(b) obligations by the licensee limiting the invention to certain uses or technical applications, limiting the quantities produced, limiting the time and/or area of exploitation, and an agreement by the licensee not to grant sub-licences; and
(c) the imposition of quality standards.

The agreement must not contain any restrictive clause other than those contained in the Notice to qualify for the negative clearance. Certain patent licensing agreements are now covered by 'bloc' exemption under Regulation 2349/84 (OJ 1984 L 219/15) (see page 164).

Some specific agreements

Exclusive distribution agreements

Simple distribution agreements, where neither the supplier nor the dealer are bound to any restrictive obligations, do not fall within Article 85 (1). But where the supplier agrees to supply only one distributor within a defined area, Article 85 (1) is relevant, as there is a restriction on competition in that the supplier is no longer free to supply other distributors, and even consumers directly, in that area. In return for the exclusive distributorship, the distributor will also normally accept certain restrictions, such as agreeing not to sell outside his area, or not to sell competing products.

Exclusive distributor agreements can, though, have certain beneficial effects. They may improve the efficiency of distribution, open up markets leading to a wider choice to consumers, and make it easier for a producer to enter new markets. This can make for an increase in competition and contribute to market unification, thus leading to increased trade between Member States. The Commission have, in practice, found many exclusive distribution agreements to have satisfied the requirements of Article 85 (3) for exemption. Therefore, to avoid having to deal with many individual applications for exemption, the Commission in 1967 put into effect a 'bloc' exemption (Regulation 67/67). Regulation 67/67 has now been replaced by two Regulations, one relating to exclusive distribution agreements (Regulation 1983/83), and the other to exclusive purchasing agreements (Regulation 1984/83), both of which came into effect on 1 July 1983. Regulation 67/67 remains in force until the end of 1986 for agreements which were in effect prior to 1984.

Regulation 1983/83 exempts two party agreements whereby one party agrees to supply goods for resale within the whole, or a defined area, of the Common Market. To qualify for exemption the agreement must not contain any restrictions other than those specified in the Regulation. These include:

(1) restrictions on the supplier not to sell to other distributors, or consumers directly within the defined area;
(2) restrictions on the distributor not to manufacture or sell competitive goods;

(3)   a restriction on the distributor to concentrate his sales efforts within the given area, and not seek customers outside that area. However, he must always be free to sell outside that area, even in those areas allocated to other distributors. Thus he can supply unsolicited orders, the restriction being not to solicit orders, except in his area;

(4)   obligations on the distributor to purchase minimum quantities or complete ranges of goods, to sell under the trade mark or packaging as indicated by the supplier, and take specific measures to promote sales.

In particular, it is provided that manufacturers of competing goods must not enter into exclusive distributor agreements with each other in respect of such goods, as this could lead to horizontal market sharing, which is always disapproved by the Commission. An exception to this prohibition has been made in respect of non-reciprocal distribution agreements, that is where one manufacturer appoints the other as his distributor, but not vice versa, if one of the parties has a turnover of not more than 100 million ECU.

Exclusive purchasing agreements

Regulation 1984/83 exempts two party agreements whereby one party agrees to buy specific goods for resale only from the other party. The agreement must not contain restrictions other than those permitted in the Regulation, which are similar to those in Regulation 1983/83. Again, there is a ban on agreements between manufacturers of competing goods, except for non-reciprocal agreements for small and medium sized businesses.

The reason for separating exclusive purchasing agreements from exclusive distribution agreements is that an agreement whereby a reseller is obliged to buy exclusively from a specified supplier poses different problems. Where a supplier has succeeded in tying many or all sales outlets in a given area, competitors find it difficult, and in some cases impossible, to enter the market. The longer the period of time, and the wider the range of products tied, the greater the barrier to market entry.

The Regulation thus provides that the maximum period for

any exclusive purchasing agreement is 5 years, and the range of products covered by the agreement must be limited to those connected to each other, either by their nature or commercial usage.

Special provisions apply to agreements relating to beer and petrol, as often these agreements often involve considerable financial involvement on the part of the supplier. The maximum duration for an agreement relating to the resale of beer or petrol is therefore increased to 10 years, or, if subject to a tenancy, for the length of the lease, if longer. The range of products for both types of supply agreement is limited, in the case of beer to other drinks, and in the case of petrol to petroleum based motor fuels. Other products, such as tobacco and car accessories, cannot be subject to the agreement if it is to fall within the exemption.

One uncertainty about the scope of both exemptions relates to the meaning of goods supplied for resale. Often the final stage of manufacture is carried out by the dealer, and it is not clear in this case if the goods are bought for resale, and thus come within the exemption. If the processing left to the dealer amounts to more than merely packaging the product, it will be safer, to be sure of being able to enforce the agreement, for the supplier to notify the Commission, and claim individual exemption.

The underlying principle behind these 'bloc' exemptions relating to exclusive distribution and purchasing agreements is, that while certain restrictions which improve distribution and open up markets will be allowed, they must not go too far. They must never result in the isolation of national markets and prevent parallel imports. The parties must not attempt to create absolute territorial protection for the distributor. Where the restrictions in the agreement will make it difficult for consumers to obtain the contract goods from other dealers by restraining parallel imports, the 'bloc' exemptions will be inapplicable and application for individual exemption will not be viewed favourably.

In *Polistil/Arbois (1984)*, an Italian manufacturer, Polistil, and its exclusive distributor in France, Arbois, were fined by the Commission for breach of Article 85 (1). The exclusive distribution agreement contained clauses under which Polistil agreed to impose a ban on its other distributors from selling in France, and to sell to Arbois at prices which would make it easier for Arbois to meet any competition. The agreement conferred absolute territorial protection to Arbois by preventing or restricting parallel imports, and was thus outside the bloc exemption.

The attitude of the Commission, and the ECJ, to attempts to prevent or restrict parallel imports can be illustrated by reference to *Consten and Grundig v EC Commission (1966)*. Grundig, a German manufacturer, made an exclusive distributor and purchasing agreement with Consten, a French distributor, giving Consten exclusive rights over the marketing of Grundig's products in France. Consten agreed not to handle competing goods, or sell outside France. Grundig, in return, promised not to sell, either directly, or indirectly through other dealers, to other distributors, or to consumers, in France.

Alongside this contract was a subsidiary arrangement whereby Consten registered the trade mark of the products in its own name. This was done so that if Consten should meet with competition from parallel imports, one way of preventing this would be to allege the infringement of the trade mark.

Later, UNEF, another French distributor, started to import Grundig products into France, which it had obtained from German dealers. Consten brought an action in the French courts claiming breach of the exclusivity clause, and infringement of trade mark. UNEF claimed that the agreement was void under Article 85 (1). Consten then notified the agreement to the Commission claiming either negative clearance or exemption.

Negative clearance was refused on the grounds that the agreement clearly came within 85 (1). In relation to the claim for exemption, the Commission stated that the agreement attempted to grant complete territorial protection by prohibiting parallel imports, and thus held that exemption could not be granted, a decision upheld by the ECJ. Any attempt to isolate markets will meet with condemnation by the Common Market competition authorities. Such agreements are in direct conflict with market integration, which is one of the main objectives of Common Market competition policy.

Selective distribution

Many manufacturers, particularly of products which are technically sophisticated, such as cars, computers and electrical consumer goods, like their products to be sold by only certain approved dealers. Given the nature of the products involved, a selective distribution system may be entirely justified, provided the selection is based on purely qualitative grounds, such as after-sales service, technically qualified staff and suitably equipped premises. These will not be subject to the competition rules.

Thus in *Demo-Studio Schmidt v EC Commission (1984)*, the plaintiff, Schmidt, ran a part-time hi-fi business. He was unable to obtain supplies of a particular product from a manufacturer, Revox, because he did not satisfy the qualitative criteria laid down by Revox, which included technical expertise and know-how, the ability to offer after-sales service, and a requirement that retailers should be open during normal business hours. The ECJ held that since the criteria did not infringe Article 85 (1) or 86, Revox could rely on them as a basis for refusing to supply its products to Schmidt. However, selective distribution scheme must not be operated in a discriminatory manner, even if, on the face of it, it is based on objective qualitative criteria. This appears to be the case whether or not the manufacturer is in a dominant position.

Often, however, further criteria are applied in the selection of dealers, and other restrictions are applied. These may fall within the 'bloc' exemptions contained in Regulations 1983 and 1984/83, but they sometimes go beyond these. The selection system may limit the number of dealers in a particular area to what the manufacturer considers the market will bear, and further, may limit commercial freedom by restricting the persons to whom sales can be made, for example, only to other approved dealers.

Nevertheless, selective distribution systems can satisfy the requirements of Article 85 (3), and so be exempted on an individual basis. Consumers can benefit from a satisfactory after-sales service and specialist information on products, which would otherwise not be available. The distribution of goods can be improved, leading to a wider market choice.

Any indication, however, that the system is being used to maintain prices by refusing to supply discount retailers, or hinder parallel imports, will prevent exemption.

In the motor vehicle sector, selective distribution systems are invariably established, and will often be exempted because they are indispensable in providing satisfactory information, adequate repair facilities, and after-sales service for consumers. In order to avoid many applications for individual exemption, the Commission has proposed a 'bloc' exemption for certain types of distribution and servicing agreements for motor vehicles.

The exemption would allow the following restrictions on the dealer:

(a)   not to sell products of other manufacturers;
(b)   not to seek custom outside the allotted area;
(c)   not to sub-contract to other dealers or repairers; and
(d)   not to supply dealers outside the distribution network.

In return, the manufacturer may restrict his freedom to appoint other dealers in the allotted area. One important provision is that price differences between Member States for the same model of car must not exceed 12½ per cent for more than 6 months, except for taxation.

Specialization agreements

These agreements involve an arrangement whereby one manufacturer concentrates on one line of production, whilst a competitor concentrates on another. They restrict competition because the parties give up their right to independently manufacture certain items. The Commission has recognized that specialization agreements can have certain economic benefits. They can lead to an improvement in production processes, a reduction in costs, and where the agreements are between small firms faced with competition from larger firms, enable them to compete more effectively on the market. Individual exemption has often been granted, provided some of the benefits are passed on to consumers, for example, lower prices, and provided the agreement does not contain restrictions not essential to the achievement of their objectives.

For example, in the *Jaz Agreement (1970)* two manufacturers of clocks, German and French companies, agreed to specialize, one on mechanical clocks and the other on electrical. They also agreed to supply each other with the specialized products. The Commission exempted the agreement because of the economic advantages and benefits to the consumer, and because the restrictions were not too wide, although the agreement eliminated competition between them, and, as they were in different Member States, the flow of trade between Member States was affected. The benefits of the agreement were the avoidance of the duplication of research and development expenses, and improved manufacturing processes leading to cost reductions. This enabled each firm to compete more effectively in the market, where larger firms were already established.

Certain specialization agreements are now subject to a 'bloc' exemption (Regulation 3604/82, replacing Regulation 2779/72) where the turnover of the parties is not more than 300 million ECU, and the market share with respect to the specialized products does not exceed 15 per cent in a substantial part of the Common Market. The exemption is thus aimed at small and medium sized firms. If the firm is part of a group, then the turnover and market share of the whole group must be taken into account.

The specialization must be reciprocal, and if only one of the parties refrains from the production of a certain item, then the agreement will not qualify for exemption. The agreement must not contain any commitment with regard to prices, nor any limitation on production. Certain obligations will be allowed, such as a non-competition clause, exclusive distribution and purchasing arrangements, and agreement regarding minimum stocks, replacement parts and provision of after-sales service.

A 'bloc' exemption regarding research and development agreements between small and medium sized firms is in the process of preparation, and is expected to be put into effect in 1985.

Industrial property rights

The laws of all countries within the Common Market give some form of protection to industrial property rights, such as patents, copyright and trade marks. A patent gives the inventor of a product the sole right to exploit the invention for a specified period of time, and copyright gives the same protection in relation to intellectual property such as books, films, video-recordings, etc. Trade marks do not prevent others producing and selling identical goods, but allow the owner of the trade mark to take action against those who market a product in a way that is likely to cause confusion with the goods produced by the owner of the trade mark.

Article 30 of the EEC Treaty provides for the elimination of restrictions which may affect the import and export of goods between Member States. This would appear to prohibit laws of Member States protecting industrial property rights where parallel imports are affected. Article 36, however, provides that the prohibition of restrictions on trade between Member States does not extend to laws necessary to protect industrial property. The Article, though, goes on to say that the restrictions must not 'constitute a means of arbitrary discrimination or a disguised restriction on trade between Member States'. Article 36 cannot be used to avoid the competition rules provided for in Articles 85 and 86. This is clear from the case of *Consten and Grundig v EC Commission (1966)*.

In this case, Consten was licensed to use the Grundig trade mark 'GINT' in France. When UNEF, another French company, began to sell Grundig products in France, Consten sought an action based on the infringement of their trade mark, alleging that Article 36 protected industrial property rights. The ECJ held that a distinction must be drawn between the existence of the rights and their exercise. The existence is protected by Article 36, but their exercise is subject to Articles 85 and 86. As there was an improper use of the trade mark to isolate the French market from parallel imports, the agreement was void under Article 85 (1).

In *Sirena v Eda (1971)*, an American company owned the trade mark in certain toilet products in Italy and Germany, and sold the Italian mark to an Italian firm, and the German mark to a German firm. The German company later started selling the products in Italy in competition to Sirena, the Italian company. Sirena brought an action for breach of its trade mark, and the Italian court referred the case to the ECJ, asking whether the competition rules prevented the holder of a trade mark registered in one Member State from prohibiting imports from another Member State. The ECJ confirmed the position that the existence of rights granted by national law is not affected, but that the exercise of the rights may be restricted by Articles 85 and 86. This exercise is in order, unless it constitutes improper exploitation.

Article 36 only allows restrictions on trade between Member States to the extent that they are necessary to protect industrial property rights. Thus once goods protected by industrial property have been legitimately marketed by the property owner or with his consent in one Member State, the importation of the goods into another Member State cannot be prevented on the basis of parallel rights in that other Member State. So in *Deutsche Grammophon v Metro-SB-Grossemarkte (1971)*, a German record manufacturer owned the rights for the protection of recordings in Germany. It granted an exclusive licence to market the records in France to a French company, Polydor. Another firm obtained a supply of records, originally marketed by Polydor, and imported them into Germany. The German company tried to prevent these imports on the grounds that his industrial property rights were infringed.

The ECJ held that the German company could not use these rights to protect itself from competition from imports of records, which had originally been sold by it, or with its consent. If manufacturers were able to use industrial property rights in this way, the objective of the Treaty relating to the free movement of goods between Member States would not be achieved. It would amount to a disguised restriction on inter-community trade.

The exercise of industrial property rights can be a breach of either Articles 85 or 86. Where an undertaking is exercising its own rights, then of course Article 85 has no application. But where the undertaking is in a dominant position, the improper exploitation of the rights may be an abuse of a dominant position. Merely to have an industrial property right does not mean in itself that a dominant position exists. The undertaking must be in a position to prevent effective competition, for it to be in a dominant position. For an abuse to take place, there must be an improper exploitation of the rights, such as charging unjustifiable higher prices, as in *Hoffman la Roche v Secretary of State for Trade and Industry (1973)*, a case brought under the UK monopoly legislation, or by unjustifiably refusing to supply.

Article 85 becomes relevant where the owner of an industrial property right allows another firm to use that right. This, in itself, does not fall within Article 85 (1). But the granting of permission to exercise industrial property rights is usually accompanied by clauses imposing some form of exclusivity and territorial protection, which can lead to the isolation of national markets. In this case, Article 85 (1) is of relevance.

Patent licensing agreements   These account for the majority of notifications to the Commission seeking negative clearance or exemption in the area of industrial property. Although they often restrict trade between Member States, patent licensing agreements do have several beneficial aspects, particularly for small firms. Such agreements can lead to a wider distribution of goods, and increased trade between Member States. Smaller firms can gain access to new technology, which they would not otherwise be able to do. Patent licensing can also encourage innovation by small firms, where they do not have the technical or financial resources to exploit the inventions themselves, particularly on a Community-wide scale.

It has been seen that two-party agreements relating to the use of industrial property rights do not have to be notifed to the Commission in order to obtain exemption, and that certain patent licensing agreements are the subject of a Notice giving 'bloc' negative clearance. There is also a 'bloc' exemption relating to patent licensing agreements under Regulation 2349/84 (OJ 1984 L 219/15).

The exemption applies only to bilateral agreements, and

will exempt from Article 85 (1) exclusive rights to manufacture and use specific products. Also exempted are exclusive selling rights, and accompanying export restrictions by small and medium sized firms, who, because of limited financial resources, have difficulty in exploiting the inventions themselves. Similar protection is given to small firms who are granted licences.

The Regulation gives a list of permitted obligations, including grant-back clauses, the respect of quality standards, field of use restrictions, and a requirement not to grant sub-licences or divulge secrets. Certain clauses in the agreement will prevent the application of the 'bloc' exemption. These include resale price fixing, competing products clauses, quantitative restrictions and a licence for an indefinite duration. It will be still open for the parties to be exempted individually, after notification to the Commission, though the Commission will have to be satisfied that there are good reasons for an exemption.

Conclusion

In the control of cartels, Article 85 is framed in very general terms. It catches all agreements which have the effect of adversely affecting competition within the Common Market. In contrast, the Restrictive Trade Practices Act is much more precisely defined in relation to the registration of restrictive trading agreements within the United Kingdom, where the restrictions must relate to the practices listed in the Act. It is therefore somewhat clearer as to whether an agreement is registrable under the United Kingdom legislation, than whether an agreement would be caught by Article 85 (1). The introduction of group exemptions has made the position clearer in many common situations, but there are still many areas where it is not possible for undertakings to be certain whether their agreements are enforceable or not.

Even where the agreement has been notified to the Commission, the parties can never be entirely sure until the Commission has reached a decision regarding exemption. Informal indications from the Commission, such as comfort letters, do not bind the national courts, although they are likely to give serious consideration to them. Even negative clearance is not a binding decision of the Commission, although it would be extremely rare for a national court to declare an agreement void once negative clearance has been given.

A further problem of Common Market competition law is its territorial reach. United Kingdom law applies the territorial principle, that is for an agreement to come within the legislation it must be between persons carrying on business in the United Kingdom. On the other hand, the Commission follows the effects theory, that is it claims jurisdiction over any undertaking, no matter where located, if its activities affect competition within the Common Market.

So in *Dyestuffs (1972)*, the Commission fined ICI, a United Kingdom company, before Britain entered the Common Market. ICI appealed to the ECJ on the grounds that the Commission had no jurisdiction over companies outside its territorial boundaries. The ECJ confirmed the fine, but on the basis that ICI was carrying on business within the Common Market through its subsidiaries. But in *Commercial Solvents (1974)*, the ECJ confirmed the Commission's view by holding that the country in which a company is registered or domiciled is irrelevant if competition in the Common Market is affected by its activities.

One final problem concerns the possibility of conflict between national and Common Market law. The Common Market competition rules do not replace the national systems of the Member States, but are applied alongside them. It is possible that a practice can therefore infringe both national and Common Market law. In such cases, it is possible that parallel proceedings may be taken by both the national and Common Market authorities. Parallel proceedings were confirmed in *Wilhelm v Bunderskartellamt (1969)*, where the company was fined by both the German Kartelamt, for breach of German competition law, and by the Commission for breach of the Common Market rules. However, the ECJ said that the Commission, when imposing a fine, should bear in mind any fines already imposed under national law.

Where there is conflict, the Common Market rules should

prevail. But this does not mean that a practice which is valid under Article 85 is therefore valid under the Restrictive Trade Practices Act. So if the Commission grant negative clearance under Article 85 on the grounds that the agreement does not affect trade between Member States, that agreement can still be declared void by the Restrictive Practices Court. On the other hand, the position is not so clear in relation to an agreement which is given an exemption because of the economic benefits, but which fails to pass through the 'gateways' under the United Kingdom legislation. In practice the possibility of conflict is slight, as the Director General has the power to refrain from referring an agreement to the Restrictive Practices Court in cases where the agreement is exempted under Article 85 (3).

9

Resale Price Maintenance

Introduction

Resale price maintenance (RPM) is the practice whereby the manufacturer of a product controls the price at which the product is sold to the public. Where the manufacturer distributes through his own retail outlets, the prices at which his products are retailed can be directly controlled. But where the manufacturer distributes through independent traders, the manufacturer cannot directly control prices and other terms of sale of those traders. However, a similar result can be achieved by the manufacturer inserting a term in the contract with the distributor, to the effect that the distributor will only resell at, or not less than, prices laid down by the manufacturer.

There are a number of arguments in favour of RPM. Where the manufacturer supplies branded goods, he has an interest in ensuring control over the distribution, as the goods are directly connected with him. RPM allows the manufacturer to fix the margins at a level which will encourage the retailer to handle and stock his products on a satisfactory scale, and to provide necessary pre- and after-sales service. It ensures that large retailers do not use their buying power to negotiate discounts, which can be used to cut prices, as this may lead to the smaller retailer not handling certain products. This is important where there is a substantial investment in advertising by the manufacturer, as it is essential that there are an adequate number of retail outlets to meet consumer response.

RPM, by protecting the manufacturer from price cutting

and granting discounts, enables him to maintain quality and protect his reputation. This is particularly true of high-priced goods, where the price can be part of the sales image of the goods. If goods are heavily discounted by retailers, this image can be lost.

The small retailer obviously benefits from RPM, as it protects him from price competition by the large retailer who is able, not only to work on smaller margins due to higher turnover, but also to negotiate lower prices from the manufacturer. The wholesaler, too, benefits, as large retailers are in a position to bypass the wholesaler and deal directly with the manufacturer. It is also claimed that consumers benefit because RPM ensures a greater number of retail outlets, and that it prevents the need to shop around to find the lowest price.

RPM is, however, anti-competitive. Fixed retail prices precludes price competition between retailers, and as the more efficient retailer cannot pass on to consumers the benefits of this greater efficiency, prices are higher than they would otherwise have been. The margins, too, are fixed at a level which keeps the less efficient trader in business. On the other hand, the reduction in retail outlets could eventually cause a reduction in competition.

It is important to distinguish between two different methods of RPM agreements, collective and individual. Collective agreements are on a horizontal level, that is, between two or more manufacturers whereby they agree with each other that they will maintain their retail prices. They each agree to enter into a number of individual RPM agreements. Individual agreements exist at a vertical level, between a manufacturer and a distributor, the latter agreeing to keep to the prices laid down by the former.

Collective RPM

Horizontal RPM agreements, which contain collective enforcement provisions, such as the power to impose fines, or the collective withholding of supplies from a distributor who cuts prices, were made unlawful under section 24 Restrictive Trade Practices Act, 1956. This provision is now contained in the Resale Prices Act, 1976. Section 1 provides that it is unlawful for any two or more persons carrying on business in the United Kingdom to make any agreement or arrangement to withhold supplies of goods, or extract penalties, from dealers who sell in breach of any RPM agreement. Section 2 provides similarly in relation to dealers who withhold orders from any supplier who breaches a RPM provision.

No criminal proceedings lie, however, for contravention of the Act. Section 25 (2) provides that compliance shall be enforceable by civil proceedings on behalf of the Crown for an injunction or other appropriate relief. Section 25 (3) provides that any person who has been affected by a contravention can take civil action for breach of statutory duty.

Horizontal agreements which do not contain collective enforcement provisions are registrable under the Restrictive Trade Practices Act, and dealt with like any other restrictive trading agreement. Thus, once registered, an agreement is referred to the Court, and if it passes through one of the 'gateways', and satisfies the balancing tailpiece, the Court can declare it valid.

Only one collective RPM agreement has satisfied the requirements of section 10 Restrictive Trade Practices Act. That was the *Net Book Agreement (No. 2) (1964)*. The Court was satisfied that without RPM, booksellers would only stock quick selling titles, as there would be no incentive to stock slower moving titles. The agreement also kept in business an adequate number of specialist bookshops, by protecting them against price cutting by other retailers. It was also considered that printing and binding costs were kept down, as RPM helped to ensure sufficient orders.

Individual RPM

Vertical RPM agreements were not adversely affected by the 1956 Act. In fact, the position of such agreements was strengthened. The doctrine of privity of contract prevented a manufacturer from directly enforcing a RPM provision against a retailer who obtained supplies from a wholesaler. This is because there is no contract between the manufacturer and retailer. In *Dunlop v Selfridges (1915),* Dunlop sold tyres to a distributor on RPM terms. The distributor then sold to Selfridges including the RPM provisions. It was held that Dunlop could not sue Selfridges because there was no contract between them.

In practice, the manufacturer, as in *Dunlop v Selfridges*, would include a term in the contract with the wholesaler, requiring the wholesaler to include a RPM condition in his contract with the retailer. Thus the contract could be enforced indirectly through the wholesaler.

The Report of the Committee on Resale Price Maintenance (Lloyd-Jacobs Committee (1949)), while condemning horizontal RPM, reported favourably on vertical agreements. They took the view that a manufacturer should be able to enforce retail prices directly against a retailer, even though there was no contract between them. The 1956 Act gave assistance to vertical agreements by enacting the Committee's recommendations. It was provided that a producer could enforce a RPM provision directly against a retailer, even where the retailer had purchased from a wholesaler. Privity of contract was abolished in relation to vertical RPM agreements.

In the next few years, the tide of opinion started to turn against vertical, as well as horizontal agreements. The argument that they restricted competition and kept prices high gained support. In any case, the practice was beginning to break down, particularly in groceries, with the growth of large, multiple retailers. Manufacturers, in many instances, could not afford to cut off supplies to the multiples, who often possessed economic power as great, if not greater, than the manufacturer. In 1964, the Resale Prices Act was passed making vertical agreements, and relating enforcement provisions unlawful, unless the Court could be persuaded by the manufacturer that RPM in respect of his products was in the public interest.

Prohibition of individual RPM

The present controls are contained in the Resale Prices Act 1976. Section 9 (1) provides that:

Any term or condition −

(a) of a contract for the sale of goods by a supplier to a dealer, or
(b) of any agreement between a supplier and a dealer relating to such a sale,

is void in so far as it purports to establish or provide for the establishment of minimum prices to be charged for the resale of goods in the United Kingdom.

Section 9 (1) only refers to minimum prices, and does not affect terms and conditions relating to maximum prices. Thus where a manufacturer produces an unbranded version of a branded product, he can lay down the maximum price of the unbranded version in order to protect his brand image. A manufacturer can also recommend the prices at which his products shall be sold. The Act, also, only refers to contracts relating to goods and not services. It is therefore possible for a tour operator to lay down the prices at which a retail travel agent should sell holidays to the public.

Section 9 (2) makes it unlawful for a supplier of goods to include any term or condition in a contract of sale, or agreement relating to the sale of goods, which is void under section 9 (1). It is also unlawful under section 11 for a supplier to withhold supplies from a dealer who sells, or is likely to sell, below the minimum price.

The Act, thus, has two effects on vertical agreements. The agreements are made void and unenforceable, and certain actions are made unlawful. As with horizontal agreements, no criminal proceedings lie, enforcement being by civil action, either on behalf of the Crown, or by an individual, such as a retailer who has had supplies withheld. For example, in *Comet v Farnell − Tandberg* (1971), the manufacturer objected to Comet advertising their products at discount prices, and withdrew supplies from Comet as they feared damage to their image. Comet sought an injunction, and this was granted on the ground that this was unlawful under what is now section 11. The manufacturer had refused to supply Comet on the grounds that the retailer was likely to sell at cut prices.

However, it is necessary to show that the reason to

withhold supplies is related to RPM, and not for some other reason, such as failing to maintain after-sales facilities. In *Oxford Printing Co. Ltd. v Letraset Ltd. (1970)*, the plaintiffs in their advertising recommended that customers using Letraset products should switch to those of a competitor. Letraset refused to sell to the plaintiffs, who sought an injunction. This was refused on the ground that there was a reason outside the Resale Prices Act for refusing to supply. (A refusal to supply which is not related to RPM may be an anti-competitive practice under the Competition Act, see Chapter 4.)

It is provided in section 11 that it is not unlawful for a manufacturer to withhold supplies of goods for a dealer, if he has reason to believe that the dealer has been using the goods as loss leaders within the preceding 12 months. Loss leaders are goods sold at a price below cost in order to attract customers into the shop, where they will hopefully buy other goods. Loss leader was described by the Lloyd-Jacobs Committee as:

> the name frequently applied to an article sold at a price cut drastically below the established retail price. It is used as a form of advertisement to attract customers into the shop in the hope that they will, at the same time, purchase articles showing a higher rate of profit, or that the increase in the turnover of articles showing a normal rate of profit will outweigh the losses sustained on sales of the leading line.

A sale of goods sold at a drastically reduced price will not be treated as a loss leader, where sold by retailers in a genuine seasonal or clearance sale.

Exemption

If a manufacturer wishes to control the prices at which his products are sold he can seek exemption under section 14. Upon application, by either the manufacturer or the manufacturers trade association, or the Director, the Court has the power to exempt goods of any class from the provisions of the Act. Section 14 establishes a procedure similar to that under Section 10 Restrictive Trade Practices Act, that is, a number of 'gateways' through one of which the agreement must pass, together with a balancing tailpiece.

To gain exemption, the manufacturer has to show that in default of a system of maintained resale prices, any of the following consequences will occur to the detriment of consumers:

(1) the quality or variety of goods available for sale would be substantially reduced;
(2) the number of retail outlets would be substantially reduced;
(3) prices in the long run would be increased;
(4) goods would be retailed under conditions likely to cause damage to health; or
(5) necessary services provided with or after the sale of the goods would either cease to be given, or be substantially reduced.

In addition, the manufacturer will have to show that any of the detriments mentioned above, will outweigh the detriment of maintaining minimum resale prices and foregoing free competition.

Exemption has been granted by the Court in only two instances, books and medicaments. Reference has been made to the *Net Book Agreement* in connection with horizontal RPM agreements. In the *Medicaments Reference (No. 2) (1970)*, the Court found that if RPM was terminated, it would lead to a reduction in retail outlets, less variety of products, and a reduction in services. Large retailers would sell only quick selling lines, thus reducing variety. With reduced prices, the number of chemists' shops would decline as they would be unable to compete. This would lead to a consequent reduction in services offered to consumers by the specialist chemist.

RPM in the Common Market

There are no specific provisions in the Common Market competition rules relating to RPM. Whether an RPM agreement is prohibited depends, therefore, on whether it is caught by Article 85 (1). The effect of an RPM provision in an agreement must be to restrict competition, as price competition between dealers is prevented. Whether an RPM agreement comes within Article 85 (1) depends, therefore, on whether there is a significant effect on trade between Member States.

It would appear to be the case that an RPM agreement between a manufacturer and a dealer, both of whom are in one Member State, and which does not contain any provision relating to imports and exports, would not be caught. If, however, the agreement contains any provision which relates to inter-community trade, the agreement would come within Article 85 (1). Thus if a manufacturer makes a provision relating to resale prices in a contract with a distributor, that can only apply to resales within that Member State. The distributor must be able to export to other Member States free of the restriction.

In *ASPA (1970)*, a trade association of Belgian perfumery manufacturers and distributors bound its members to enforce RPM for goods they manufactured or imported, and made provision for a collective boycott. The Commission held that the agreement restricted competition in the supply of imported perfumery products, and affected trade between Member States as it was difficult to bypass the distribution channels of the association.

Similarly, an agreement between a manufacturer in one Member State and a distributor in another, would also be caught. In *Hennessey/Henkel (1981)*, a French manufacturer had an RPM agreement relating to Cognac with its exclusive dealer in Germany. Although the agreement contained no export restrictions, and there was price competition between other brands, the agreement was condemned by the Commission.

In assessing whether there is a significant effect on trade between Member States, the RPM system as a whole must be considered, and not each individual agreement separately. In *Brasserie de Haecht v Wilkin & Wilkin (1968)*, it was held by the ECJ that other related agreements must be taken into consideration.

Vertical RPM agreements between two parties are excused from notification under Article 4 of Regulation 17, where the sole restriction is that which relates to prices and terms of resale. This does not mean that the agreement is valid, but merely that the Commission can grant exemption or negative clearance without notification.

Conclusion

The practice of RPM, which once covered a wide range of goods and services in the United Kingdom, has been virtually eradicated, at least in relation to goods, by the Resale Prices Act, and the policy of the Court. RPM now covers only two areas, books and certain pharmaceutical products, and accounts for less than 2 per cent of consumer expenditure. Nevertheless, there is some evidence that RPM is operating through the 'back door', and that certain manufacturers refuse to supply goods for resale to discount retailers in order to protect the image of their product against price cutting. The reasons given for this refusal are usually based on other criteria, but the suspicion sometimes remains that the real reason is the feared damage to the reputation of the manufacturer when his products are heavily discounted.

In 1982, the Office of Fair Trading received over thirty complaints alleging contravention of the Resale Prices Act, covering a wide range of goods. In the majority of cases no evidence was found to justify taking action, but in one case undertakings were taken from one supplier not to breach the Act, and in a number of other cases the Office suggested amendments to sales literature to prevent misunderstanding on pricing policies.

The Act has been successful in freeing markets from price control by manufacturers, leading to lower prices and wider consumer choice. But there is growing concern over the decline of the small retailer, particularly in food retailing, and in villages. Those who survive have to charge higher prices than the large retailer operating super- and hyper-markets. The growing trend for out of town stores, often not on regular public transport routes means that those who do not have their own transport, often the elderly, have to pay the higher prices in the small shops which have so far survived.

The Office of Fair Trading has recently started an enquiry to discover whether large retailers are unfairly pressurizing food manufacturers to give bigger discounts.

This follows complaints from the manufacturers that they have been threatened that unless they increase discounts they will be 'blacklisted'. Small retailers have also complained, in that they are being forced out of business because they cannot get the same terms as the supermarkets.

In a Monopolies and Mergers Commission Report (1981) the Commission found that the discounts were beneficial to competition, and not against the public interest. This new investigation is to see if the position has changed, and to discover if there is enough evidence to justify another Commission investigation.

There are a number of actions which could be taken. In the first place, there is a case for more products to be subject to RPM, and exempted under section 14. Secondly, the Director could make an investigation to see if the pricing policies of some manufacturers, or the pressure applied by some retailers for larger discounts, amount to anti-competitive practices under the Competition Act. Finally, there is some case for the introduction of legislation providing a remedy against unfair competition on the German lines. This would enable the small shop, facing intense competition from the large retailer, to bring a legal action if that competition is unfair. The small retailer has a difficult enough task competing against the lower costs of the large multiples without facing further pressure from discrimination.

10

Public Enterprise and State Aid

Introduction

In the United Kingdom, as in most western democracies, the state is closely involved in industry and commerce. This involvement has important implications for competition law and policy, as the state is in a favourable position in relation to private undertakings, and is in a position to create monopolies or grant monopoly powers, and other competitive advantages.

This state involvement can take various forms. In the first place the state directly controls large parts of the economy through its ownership of public undertakings. Often the state grants monopoly powers to these public undertakings and competition by private firms is prohibited by law. This is particularly true in the field of energy, transport and communications. Even in those instances where competition is allowed, the favourable position of a state enterprise can place it at a competitive advantage to competing firms, and they often enjoy dominant positions within the market.

Even where the state does not take an enterprise into public ownership, it can grant a monopoly to a private undertaking. In the United States, it is more common to give firms engaged in providing public utility services, such as gas and electricity, a monopoly rather than take them into public ownership. The present trend in the United Kingdom towards 'privatization' will mean a larger number of privately owned monopolies, such as British Telecom, with their monopoly powers guaranteed by law.

Finally there is the question of state aids, both to public

and private enterprises. These can take many forms such as direct subsidies, tax benefits and incentives, provision of capital and various regional and development grants among others. These forms of state aid, by favouring some undertakings or business sectors can have the effect of distorting competition by placing those organizations which receive aid at a competitive advantage.

The involvement of the state in business is more likely to cause problems in connection with Common Market than with United Kingdom competition policy and law. Policy within the United Kingdom can have the effect of distorting competition where the state provides assistance to undertakings over which it has control, when the same assistance is not provided for competitors. For example, the three largest air charter carriers in the private sector fear that the highly competitive market will be upset by what they describe as unfair competition from the British Airways charter subsidiary, British Airtours. British Airtours is planning to take delivery of a number of aircraft from its parent, British Airways, at a price much below market rates. These aircraft were orginally bought with the help of state subsidies and loans. British Airtours will thus have a competitive edge over its rivals. The main problem lies in ensuring that the public undertakings do not abuse their monopoly or dominant market situations, act in a manner contrary to the public interest, or engage in various anti-competitive practice.

The main concern in connection with state involvement in business is in relation to Common Market competition policy. State monopolies and public undertakings are in a strong position to erect barriers to entry into a national market by competitors from other Member States. This is particularly so where the state itself guarantees the monopoly. The effect of this is to prevent or restrict inter-community trade by the prevention of parallel imports. The use of state aids to support undertakings in one Member State places those undertakings in a favourable competitive position in relation to undertakings from other Member States who do not enjoy the aids. This can again affect trade between Member States, and so distort competition within the Common Market.

The United Kingdom position

Monopoly reference

Section 2 (1) of the Monopoly and Restrictive Practices Act 1948 excluded the reference to the MMC of the activities of public corporations engaged in trading, mainly the nationalized industries. As this exclusion does not appear in the Fair Trading Act, nationalized industries and other public bodies are now subject to reference to, and investigation by, the Commission.

The Director himself has limited powers of reference. He can only refer a nationalized industry to the MMC provided it is not involved in the provision of goods or services listed in Schedules 5 and 7 of the Act. These include the supply of gas and electricity, road and rail passenger transport, postal and telephone services, television and radio, the supply of water, air transport, port facilities and certain specified agricultural products. Thus the Director was able to refer the supply of domestic gas appliances to the MMC for an investigation, even though the monopoly supplier was the British Gas Corporation, a nationalized industry.

Where the goods and services which are the subject of a reference are those listed in Schedules 5 and 7, the reference can only be made by the secretary of state, and even he cannot act alone, but only in conjunction with the appropriate minister. This is provided for in section 51 (2) which provides that where it appears that a monopoly situation exists, and the goods or services in question are of a description specified in Schedules 5 or 7, the secretary of state shall not make a reference with respect to that situation except jointly with another minister. This places the power to refer nationalized industries into the political arena for the most part, and as no references have yet been made under the section, the bringing into monopoly control of the state controlled undertakings has had no practical impact.

Public body reference

The power to investigate the activities of the nationalized industries has been widened by the Competition Act 1980, which allows for public body references. Section 11 (1) authorizes the secretary of state to refer to the MMC questions relating to:

(a)   the efficiency and costs of;
(b)   the service provided by; or
(c)   the possible abuse of a monopoly situation by;

most public bodies, including the nationalized industries which supply goods or services, water authorities, boards administering agricultural schemes, and operators of bus services.

The procedure follows closely that of a monopoly reference. The MMC must investigate and report on any question referred to it, except for questions relating to the appropriateness of any financial obligations, or guidance as to financial objectives imposed on the undertaking by the Government. The MMC is thus prevented from criticizing a nationalized industry where it is being used as an instrument of economic policy. This would include price increases forced on a nationalized industry, to raise revenue, such as those imposed on the British Gas Corporation, or price suppression as a counter-inflation policy. Also excluded is any criticism of conduct relating to a registrable restrictive trading agreement.

The reference may be limited to the facts, that is the MMC is only asked to report on the factual questions asked of it, and is not asked to report on the public interest. In the National Coal Board reference (1982) the MMC was asked to 'investigate and report on the question whether the Board could improve its efficiency and thereby reduce its costs'. No question was asked relating to the public interest. In such a case, no subsequent action can be taken on the report under the Act, though no doubt the matter will be referred to the appropriate minister. So in the Anglian and North West Water Authorities reference, where the MMC concluded that neither Authority was pursuing a course of conduct contrary to the public interest, the secretary of state announced that the recommendations to improve efficiency would be followed up by the Minister for Environmental Services.

Most public body references have been public interest

references. Here the MMC is asked to report not only on the facts, but also whether the undertaking is pursuing a course of conduct which operates against the public interest. Where the MMC has concluded that a public body is engaged in a course of conduct against the public interest, the secretary of state, or the appropriate minister, can direct the body concerned to prepare a plan to remedy the adverse public interest effects. This plan when completed must be laid before Parliament.

The secretary of state can also exercise any of the powers provided in Schedule 8, Fair Trading Act (see Chapter 3), with the exception of those relating to price regulation. The secretary of state has therefore no powers to make an order preventing discriminatory or predatory pricing, or to order a reduction in prices where excess profits are being made. The plan provisions, however, allow for the alteration of the undertakings pricing structure in the plan presented to the minister.

The power to make a public body reference is vested solely in the secretary of state, and unlike a monopoly reference under section 51, Fair Trading Act, he does not have to act jointly with another minister. The reference of public bodies remains political, though, as the Director has no jurisdiction. This has led to the fear that public body references will be used in the main for highly publicized efficiency studies to meet criticisms of certain nationalized industries (Cunningham, 1980).

To a certain extent these fears have proved to be justified so far. Most of the public body references which have so far been made have related to the question of efficiency and costs, and only rarely has the MMC been asked to report on the possible abuse of a monopoly situation. These instances have been confined to investigations into the activities of passenger transport undertakings, as in the Local Bus Undertakings reference (1981) and the Caledonian MacBrayne Ltd. reference (1982).

Competition reference

Public bodies and nationalized industries can, in the course of their activities, carry out an anti-competitive practice, if the activities are carried on for gain or reward, or in the course of which it supplies goods or services otherwise than free of charge. A nationalized industry is, therefore, like any undertaking, subject to be investigated by the Director, and a competition reference to the MMC. The only power available to the secretary of state is one of veto, which he must exercise within two weeks. Both the London Electricity Board and the British Railways Board have been investigated by the Director under section 3 of the Act for engaging in courses of conduct suspected of being anti-competitive practices (see Chapter 9).

Common Market position

Public undertakings

It is made clear by Article 90 (1) of the EEC Treaty that nationalized industries are subject to the competition rules of the Common Market. The Article provides that 'public undertakings and undertakings to which Member States grant special or exclusive rights' are bound by Articles 85 and 86. Public undertakings, and other undertakings which have been granted special rights and privileges, are thus placed in the same competitive position as private enterprise. Member States are prohibited by Article 90 (1) from making new rules, or retaining old ones, which enable these undertakings engage in restrictive practices or abuse their dominant position in the market.

Article 90 (2), however, provides for two exceptions to the general prohibition contained in 90 (1). These are 'undertakings entrusted with the operation of services of general economic interest, or having the character of a revenue producing monopoly'. The first category contains those undertakings which are engaged in the provision of some public utility service, such as the supply of electricity, gas, or water. The ECJ has held, in *Sacchi (1974)*, that a television undertaking operating under statutory powers came within the exception.

The second category covers various state revenue raising monopolies, more usual in the rest of the Common Market than in the United Kingdom. They include those engaged in the production of a variety of goods including salt, matches, tobacco, alcohol and explosives. Private undertakings can also come under Article 90 (2) provided they have been entrusted with the performance of a service by the state.

Article 90 (2) provides however that the exemption from the competition rules will only apply to the extent that the application of them will obstruct the performance of the tasks assigned to the undertaking. Thus, if a public undertaking engages in restrictive action which is not necessary to the performance of its duties, then it will fall outside the exception contained in Article 90 (2). Thus, in *British Telecom (1983)* the Commission held that the limits placed by British Telecom on telex forwarding were an abuse of a dominant position. The Commission accepted that British Telecom was entrusted with services of general economic interest, and was therefore an undertaking to which Article 90 (2) applied. The prevention of other message forwarding agencies in the United Kingdom from undercutting telex tariffs would not, however, obstruct the performance of the particular tasks ascribed by the state to British Telecom.

Under Article 90 (3) the Commission is empowered to ensure that the competition rules are applied to public, as well as private, undertakings. This is done by addressing appropriate directives or decisions to Member States. These directives or decisions can be specific, that is addressed to a particular Member State in relation to its dealings with a particular undertaking, or general, that is addressed to all Member States.

The authority of the Commission to lay down a general directive was confirmed by the ECJ in *France, Italy and United Kingdom v Commission (1980)*. The Commission passed a Directive on the transparency of financial relations between Member States and public undertakings. This Directive gives the power to the Commission to examine the financial position between a Member State and public enterprises. The three countries objected that Article 90 (3) only gave the Commission the power to issue a Directive or a decision to a particular Member State, and it did not give the Commission the power to legislate. That could only be done by the Council. However, the ECJ upheld the validity of the Directive.

There is some doubt as to how far a decision can be addressed to the undertaking itself under Regulation 17, as Article 90 (3) only allows the Commission to address a directive or a decision to a Member State. The view appears to be that where a public undertaking has committed a breach of the competition rules acting independently, then Regulation 17 can be used to address a decision to the undertaking concerned. But where the public undertaking is acting under instructions from the Member State, then the Commission should address the decision to the Member State and not to the undertaking itself. Italy has in fact commenced proceedings before the ECJ for the annulment of the decision addressed to British Telecom on the grounds that the Commission should have acted under Article 90 (3) as British Telecom were not acting independently, but applying rules laid down by legislation.

State aids

Competition in the Common Market can be distorted by Member States giving favoured treatment to certain enterprises, both public and private, by way of state aids. This distortion of competition can take place in two ways. It can place some undertakings in a competitively advantageous position compared with undertakings from other Member States, and it can attract undertakings to establish their business in one Member State rather than another. In times of recession and high unemployment, there is a tendency for state aids to increase, as Member States step in to protect trade and industry in their own country. So, in 1982, the Commission took decisions on 233 state aid schemes, far more than in any previous year.

Not all state aid schemes are incompatible with the Common Market. As the Commission has acknowledged in the Twelfth Report on Competition Policy (1983), the grant of state aids may often be of benefit to the Community in so far as the assistance 'favours economic growth, improves regional structures, reduces regional imbalances, and promotes research and development'. Of the aid proposals considered by the Commission in 1982, 104 were considered compatible with the Common Market.

Forms of aid

Article 92 (1) of the Treaty provides that any aid granted by a Member State, or through State resources of any form which distorts or threatens to distort competition, by favouring certain undertakings or certain market sectors, is incompatible with the Common Market in so far as it effects trade between Member States, unless the Treaty provides otherwise. The main Treaty exceptions are in the field of transport, agriculture and national security, the discussion of which is outside the scope of this book (see Lasok, 1980).

The Article does not make any attempt to define what is meant by aid. Therefore it covers all forms of state aid, whether direct or indirect. So as well as direct government grants and subsidies, it also includes such things as cheap loans, loan guarantees, tax concessions, the provision of goods and services on preferential terms, and any other measure having an equivalent effect.

The effect of the aid must be to distort, or threaten to distort competition, and affect trade between Member States, otherwise the aid does not come under Article 92 (1). There have been few instances where state aid has not fallen within the Article. One example was aid granted to craft businesses, where the Commission considered that the aid would have little, if any, effect on inter-community trade, and thus held the aid fell outside the criteria. Normally, however, state aid, even to small firms, is liable to distort competition and have an effect on trade between Member States.

Article 92 (2) and (3) then go on to provide that certain types of aid are compatible, or may be treated as compatible, with the Common Market.

Certain types of aid which are deemed to be automatically compatible with the Common Market are provided for in Article 92 (2). These are those which:

(1) have a social character, and which is granted to individual consumers, provided that there is no

discrimination regarding the origin of the products concerned;

(2) are intended to make good damage caused by natural disasters or other extraordinary events; and

(3) are provided for certain regions of Germany to compensate for disadvantages caused by the divisions of Germany.

State aids which may be treated as compatible with the Common Market are listed in Article 92 (3). These are those which:

(1) promote the economic development of areas where there is an abnormally low standard of living or serious unemployment;

(2) promote the execution of an important European project;

(3) remedy a serious disturbance in the economy of a Member State;

(4) facilitate the development of certain economic activities or areas, provided that such aid does not adversely affect trading conditions to an extent contrary to the common interest; and

(5) support other categories as may be specified by the Council acting on a proposal by the Commission.

Further, under Article 93, the Council, on application from a Member State, can authorize an aid scheme, if it is considered justified by exceptional circumstances.

Control of State aids

State aids are automatically prohibited, but subject to control by the Commission. This control is provided for in Article 93, which imposes a duty on the Commission to keep under review all aid granted by Member States, and which provides a procedure for the enforcement of state obligations with respect to aid.

Under Article 93 (3), Member States are under an obligation to notify the Commission of any plans to introduce new aid schemes, or to alter existing ones. The

Commission has 2 months in which to consider whether the scheme is compatible with the Common Market. In examining the scheme, the Commission must look at the aid as a whole and in its economic setting, paying regard to Article 92 (1) that aids which interfere with competition and affect trade between Member States are not allowed unless they fall within one of the exemptions. For the aid to be exempted, it must be, not only in the national interest, but also in the Community's interest.

The Commission takes a more favourable view on aid to the small business sector, than to larger companies. The Commission recognizes the important part played by small firms in economic growth and employment creation, and their contribution to maintaining competition in both national and community markets. Smaller firms face certain handicaps, such as access to finance, and the lack of technical resources for research and development. Their costs of production may often be higher because of their small size. However, the aid must normally contribute towards new investment or the creation of new jobs, and not merely keeping in operation uncompetitive businesses.

Where the Commission consider that the scheme is compatible with the Common Market, then the Member State is informed that the scheme can go ahead. If, however, the Commission feel that the scheme should not be authorized then the procedure under Article 93 (2) is initiated. Under this procedure the Commission must give the Member State a specific period, often one month, to defend the scheme. Representations are invited from other Member States and interested parties, the final decision of the Commission taking into account the arguments of the Member State together with the comments received from other Member States and the interested parties.

The Commission can decide whether to now approve the scheme, or to order the Member State to abandon or alter it. A Member State, if it disagrees with the Commission's decision, can appeal to the ECJ for a judicial review. The Member State is under a duty to comply with the decisions of the Commission, and should it fail to do so, then the Commission, or another Member State, can bring an enforcement action before the ECJ. Thus in *EC Commission v United Kingdom (1977)*, the United Kingdom proposed a subsidy to pig breeders on a temporary basis. The Commission considered it incompatible with the Common Market under Article 92 (1), and initiated the Article 93 (2) procedure. The United Kingdom applied to the Council under 93 (3) to authorize the scheme. When the United Kingdom refused to terminate the scheme, pending the Council's decision, the Commission brought an enforcement action, which the ECJ upheld, although its opinion was reserved on the substance of the case. The subsidy was, however, actually paid in the end as it was approved by the Council under Article 93 (3).

Under Article 93 (1), the Commission is under a duty to keep all existing aid schemes under review. If the Commission considers that an aid scheme is no longer compatible with the Common Market, then the Member State is asked to abandon or modify the scheme in line with the Commission's recommendations. Failure to comply with the recommendations can lead to the initiation of the Article 93 (2) procedure. However, unlike a new scheme, the Member State can continue with the aid until the Commission has come to a final decision.

Conclusion

The role and involvement of the state in industry and trade, either directly or indirectly, presents one of the main problems for competition law. The conferring of monopoly powers by the state on both public and private enterprises obviously has the effect of restricting and preventing competition, whilst the granting of various state aids may distort competition. The problem for competition is how to effectively exercise control over these state powers, as in the words of the EC Commission 'maintenance of undistorted competition is one of the fundamental principles of the free market economy'.

As has been seen, the control over state monopolies and other public undertakings in the United Kingdom is still largely in the hands of politicians. Thus only the Secretary of State, either acting alone or jointly with another minister, can make a public body reference, or a monopoly reference with regard to the majority of nationalized industries or state monopolies. The Director has no jurisdiction, though he can make a competition reference.

It is generally accepted that competition in the supply of goods or services provided by most of the public utilities would be wasteful, and that to grant one undertaking a monopoly can have public benefits. But even in the private sector, monopoly as such is not condemned, only the abuse of monopoly power. There is a strong case for giving the Director the power to make a monopoly or public body reference of a nationalized industry where he suspects the undertaking is abusing a monopoly position, thus taking these references out of the political arena to a certain extent.

With regard to the Common Market, competition law and policy in relation to the involvement of the state has the objective of preventing Member States from preventing, restricting or distorting competition by giving favoured treatment to certain undertakings, whether public or private. Thus under Article 90, public undertakings are brought within the competition controls, and under Article 93, state aids are prohibited if they distort competition. However, it is recognized that the free play of competition does not always achieve economic or social objectives. Thus to provide for the rationalization of struggling sectors, the development of new technologies, the implementation of social policies, or redressing regional imbalances, a Member State may be required to step in and provide assistance in some way. Both Articles 90 and 93, as discussed earlier, provide for exemptions to the general position, and allow a Member State to intervene in certain cases.

The Commission has in some instances laid down guidelines for identifying state aid which is in line with the interests of the Common Market as a whole, particularly to encourage restructuring and industrial redeployment. Detailed guidelines are in existence for regional aid, environmental aid, and certain industrial sectors including shipbuilding, steel and textiles. The Commission has also stressed that the small business is essential to the competitive structure of the Common Market, and aid programmes for this sector will be favourably looked at. The important factor when examining aid schemes is that the interests of the Community must come before the interests of a Member State. Thus state involvement will normally be acceptable if objectives of a common interest are pursued, such as research, job creation or energy saving, and also form part of an industrial or regional programme geared to Community priorities.

11

Anti-trust in the United States and West Germany

Introduction

Most developed countries have some forms of control over restrictive trading agreements and other forms or anti-competitive behaviour. It is therefore desirable to describe in outline the competition laws of the United States and West Germany, being leading trading and industrial nations, both of which have anti-trust policies which are different from, and which can usefully be contrasted with, those of the United Kingdom.

United States

Whereas in most countries, legislation to promote competitive behaviour was not enacted until the middle of the twentieth century, anti-trust legislation in the United States goes back to the nineteenth century. It thus has a much lengthier history than anti-trust in other countries.

The philosophy underlying United States competition policy can be illustrated by reference to the comments of the Supreme Court in *Northern Pacific Railway Inc. v United States (1958)*, where is was stated that:

It rests on the premise that the unrestrained interaction of competitive forces will yield the best allocation of economic resources, the lowest prices, the highest quality and the greatest material progress, while at the same time providing an environment conducive to the preservation of our democratic political and social institutions.

The basis of anti-trust law is the Sherman Act (1890), which has been supplemented by other statutes, notably the Clayton Act (1914), the Federal Trade Commission Act (1914) and the Anti-Trust Improvements Act (1976).

Sherman Act

The Act attacks two types of anti-competitive behaviour by business. Section 1 provides that 'every contract, combination . . . or conspiracy in restraint of trade or commerce among the several states or with foreign nations is hereby declared to be illegal'. By section 2 it is provided that 'every person who shall monopolize, or attempt to monopolize, or combine or conspire with any other person to monopolize any part of trade or commerce' shall be guilty of a criminal offence.

Section 1 of the Act is directed at agreements. An express agreement is, however, not required to create a contract in restraint of trade. Contracts can be implied by the conduct of the parties, so that the mere discussion of prices with a competitor taken together with parallel pricing would be a violation of the Act.

The Act makes no attempt to define the type of restrictive agreement which is illegal. Thus every contract in restraint of trade is caught, whether or not the contract has beneficial effects. In some instances, unfettered free competition can actually operate against the public interest. However, decisions of the courts have to some extent mitigated against the all-embracing words of the Act.

Many activities which on the face of it appear to violate the Sherman Act are not illegal unless they unreasonably restrain competition. This is known as the so-called 'rule of reason', which was applied in *Standard Oil v United States (1911)*. In this case the defendants were charged with conspiring to restrain trade in petroleum products and with monopolizing trade in those products. The court held that contracts in restraint of trade were illegal only if they constituted unreasonable restraints of trade. Acts which the Act prohibits may therefore be legal by a finding of fact that they are reasonable. The defendants in the case were, however, found guilty because they had acted unreasonably.

Later cases have restricted this 'rule of reason' approach. Violations of the Act have been divided into two categories, those which are illegal *per se*, and those which are illegal only if unreasonable, the rule of reason only applying to breaches in the latter category. In *National Society of Professional Engineers v United States*, the court stated that:

There are, thus, two complementary categories of anti-trust analysis. In the first category are agreements whose nature and necessary effect are so plainly anti-competitive that no elaborate study of the industry is necessary to establish their illegality − they are illegal *per se*; in the second category are agreements whose anti-competitive effect can only be evaluated by analysing the facts peculiar to the business, the history of the restraint, and the reasons why it was imposed.

Whether a particular restraint is illegal *per se* or not depends on whether it is ancillary of non-ancillary. An ancillary restraint is said to be that which is effected in furtherance of some other main object, which is not anti-competitive, although the restraint may be. Thus, territorial restrictions imposed in sole distributor agreements are not illegal *per se*, but only if they are unreasonable, as the territorial restrictions are not the main purpose of the agreement.

In the case of non-ancillary restraints, the main object of the agreement is to restrict competition, and thus they are as a matter of law unreasonable. The most common example of an agreement that is automatically illegal is one to fix prices. In *United States v Trenton Potteries (1927)*, a number of companies operated a price fixing agreement in the market for bathroom fitments. When prosecuted, they defended the agreement on the grounds that the prices were reasonable, and that there were benefits to the public from the price fixing. The Court held the agreement was illegal, stating that:

The aim of every price-fixing agreement . . . is the elimination of one form of competition. The power to fix prices, whether reasonably exercised or not, involves the power to control the market and to fix arbitrary and unreasonable prices. The reasonable price fixed for today may . . . become the unreasonable price of tomorrow.

Other practices which have been held to be as a matter of law unreasonable, and therefore not subject to an analysis of the activity to determine its reasonableness, include market sharing, collective boycotts and limitations on supply.

Section 2 of the Sherman Act is aimed at monopolization. The offence of monopoly has two elements, the possession of monopoly power, and the wilful acquisition or maintenance of that power.

For the possession of monopoly power, the Act does not specify any particular market share, though normally 75 per cent has generally been held to be necessary for there to be a monopoly. The important factors are the ability to determine price without reference to competition, and the power to erect barriers to entry into the market. Reference must also be made to the relevant market, as in United Kingdom and Common Market monopoly controls. This depends on the nature of the product and the elasticity of demand for that product, and the geographical area over which the power is exercised.

The Act does not prohibit monopoly itself, but monopolization, that is following a course of conduct to acquire or maintain monopoly power. Therefore it is not monopolization where a monopoly is created through greater efficiency, a superior product, the exercise of a patent or franchise, or even historical accident, unless steps are taken to protect or extend the monopoly. Monopolization can therefore be defined as the wilful acquisition of monopoly power by a course of deliberate conduct which is aimed at keeping other firms out of the market or from increasing their market share. The course of conduct can be any activity which is in restraint of trade.

Enforcement

The Sherman Act contains four ways of enforcing the prohibitions. In the first place it is a criminal offence, punishable by fine and/or imprisonment for any person to violate its provisions. Prosecutions can only be brought by the Department of Justice.

Secondly, the courts are empowered to grant injunctions to prevent continued violations of the Act at the request of either the Department of Justice, or a private party. As well as preventing anti-competitive behaviour, an injunction in monopoly cases can also require divestiture, that is the breaking up of the monopoly. The aim of an injunction in monopoly cases is to prevent the monopoly from enjoying the benefits of the monopoly and to render the power impotent by restoring competition. Failure to obey an injunction leads to proceedings for contempt.

Thirdly, persons who have been injured by violations of the Act can bring an action for damages. The amount of damages which can be awarded are three times the actual loss suffered, and thus amount to a punishment on the defendant as well as compensation to the injured party. Both competitors and injured members of the general public can bring an action for damages. An action for damages and/or an injunction by a private party is the most important and common remedy, and it enables action to be taken where the Government agencies have failed to do so.

Lastly, any property which is being transported from one state to another and which is owned in violation of section 1 is subject to seizure and forfeiture by the Government, though this remedy has rarely been used.

A further remedy has been added by the Anti-Trust Improvements Act (1976). It authorizes State attorneys-general to sue on behalf of consumers injured by violations of the Sherman Act, and collect triple damages for distribution to injured consumers.

Other legislation

Clayton Act (1914) Although the Sherman Act constitutes a formidable weapon in controlling anti-competitive practices, it has some inadequacies. It is written in general terms and lacks specificity. Each suspected violation has to be treated on a case by case basis on its own merits. It does little to prevent practices which only tend to reduce competition, or which are merely conducive to creating monopolies. It does not apply to practices which are likely to lead to the destruction of competition, but which fall short of an actual monopoly or combination in restraint of trade, particularly where the rule of reason applies. Further, the Act applied to situations which were never intended, such as labour unions.

The Clayton Act specifies in detail certain practices which are deemed to be anti-competitive, whether or not they are contracts, combinations or conspiracies in restraint of trade, or constitute actual monopolization or attempts to monopolize. The listed practices also do not have to actually damage competition. They are prohibited if the effect might be to substantially reduce competition or might lead to a monopoly situation.

The Act declares unlawful price discrimination, leases, sales, or contracts with tie-in or exclusive dealing terms, and interlocking directorships, where the purpose or effect is to substantially lessen competition, or tend to create a monopoly.

Section 2, on price discrimination, proved to be largely ineffective as it was drawn in too narrow terms. In particular the provision that 'discrimination in price . . . (due to) differences in the grade, quality, or quantity of the commodity sold, or that makes . . . allowance for the differences in the cost of selling or transportation' was not illegal, so weakened section 2, that it became almost impossible to prevent price discrimination.

As a result, the Act was amended in 1936 by the Robinson–Patman amendment. The aim of the amendment is to ensure equality of price to all customers where the result of unequal prices may be to substantially lessen competition or tend to create a monopoly. The amendment forbids any person engaged in commerce to discriminate in price where the goods are sold for resale. It does not, therefore, apply to a sale to a consumer, except to the extent that the lower price is justified by reason of lower transaction costs to the seller.

Violations of the Clayton Act are not crimes. The Department of Justice can obtain injunctions to prevent violations, and persons injured by a breach of the provisions can claim triple damages. The Federal Trade Commission (FTC) is also authorized to enforce the provisions of the Act.

Federal Trade Commission Act (1914)   This Act established the FTC, which is charged with the enforcement of the Clayton Act. It also has the role of overseeing the competitive process, in order to have an independent agency charged with keeping competition free and fair. In carrying out this role, it is given several functions. It gives advice on matters affecting the competitive structure, both to the government, the public and to firms seeking advice. It has the power to investigate practices which may be harmful to competition, and can gather and compile information concerning the organization and business practices of any firm engaged in commerce or industry. It also has the powers to seek information from business, and can examine witnesses and inspect documents.

In addition, the FTC enforces section 5 of the Act. This, as amended, makes unfair or deceptive acts or practices in commerce unlawful, and it can prohibit a particular business activity if it amounts to an unfair method of competition. Although charged with the duty of overseeing the competition policy of the United States, it has no powers to enforce the Sherman Act, which remains with the Department of Justice.

Mergers

Unlike the United Kingdom, the United States has a strong policy against mergers, particularly horizontal ones. The Sherman Act, under sections 1 and 2, forbids any merger between competitors if the effect of the merger would be the elimination of competition between them. The law does not allow any exemptions from this prohibition, for example, if the merger would have positive public benefits, such as economies of scale and lower prices, or to save a failing business. The reason for prohibiting horizontal mergers of this kind is to protect the public interest in a competitive market structure.

The factors which the courts will examine in determining the legality of horizontal mergers in Sherman Act cases are market share, the degree of concentration, the vulnerability of other competitors and the effects on competition. A horizontal merger is presumed to be illegal if it produces a firm having an undue percentage of the relevant market, and results in a significant increase in the concentration of firms in that market.

Section 7 of the Clayton Act, as amended, provides that no firm engaged in commerce shall acquire any of the stock or assets of any other firm, if the effect will be to substantially reduce competition, or tend to create a monopoly. As originally provided, section 7 only applied to horizontal mergers where there was an acquisition of stock. It is clear, however, that the acquisition of assets can have the same effect, and that vertical and conglomerate mergers can also have an adverse effect on competition. Since the amendment, it is clear that vertical mergers come under the Act, but there is some debate on whether conglomerate mergers are covered, but all cases have so far been settled by consent prior to a decision of the Supreme Court.

Horizontal mergers which breach the Sherman Act are enforced in the normal way under the Act, as previously discussed. Section 7 is enforced by the Department of Justice, the FTC and by individuals seeking damages. The Department of Justice can obtain an injunction to prohibit a merger, while the FTC can prevent a merger by issuing a cease and desist order, or by ordering divestiture. The powers of both the Department of Justice and the FTC are discretionary, and they have in fact issued guidelines as to which mergers are likely to be challenged.

In spite of the powers already available to the authorities, there is a feeling that there is need for additional anti-merger control. Proposed legislation is before Congress, and its advocates contend that there are many undesirable social consequences of large mergers, particularly the conglomerate type, even though the effect on competition is limited, and thus they are not illegal under either the Sherman or Clayton Acts.

The proposals would totally prohibit mergers between companies above a certain size based on assets or turnover. Other large companies would have to show that a merger would be pro-competitive before a merger would be cleared, and also show clear economic benefits to the general public. It is, however, doubtful if the law will be passed, as there is much opposition, particularly if applied to United States multinationals making it more difficult for them to compete in international markets.

State and federal law

The various anti-trust measures generally only apply if inter-state trade is effected. However, this requirement has almost been interpreted out of the legislation by the courts, and it seems that it will be satisfied even if only one state is effected provided that competition is substantially effected. Most states also have their own anti-trust legislation, but these are in fact rarely invoked, though officials in some states are more active than in others.

This is because of the wide interpretation given to inter-state trade, and because the federal law usually offers more effective remedies. Also, since the Anti-trust Improvements Act (1976), state officials can bring an action under the law on behalf of consumers injured by breaches of the legislation. The federal anti-trust laws do not apply in any state in relation to activities which are required or authorized by state law.

West Germany

The competition laws of West Germany provide a complete contrast to those of both the United States and the United Kingdom, though they have many similarities to Common Market competition law. The law is contained in the Gesetz gegen Wettbewerbsbeschränkungen (1957) (GWB) (Law against restraints in Competition). The GWB has been amended several times, the most recent being in 1980. West Germany has one of the strictest competition policies in the world, and the most comprehensive and extensive in Europe.

The main enforcement agency is the Bundeskartellamt (Federal Cartel Office), which has very wide powers given to it. The Cartel Office has considerable powers of investigation in order to obtain information, including the searching of premises, the seizing of documents and taking evidence from witnesses. It can exact fines for breaches of the law, and prohibit the implementation of restrictive agreements, prevent mergers and forbid firms from abusing a dominant position in the market. The Cartel Office acts in a quasi-judicial manner, and its decisions are subject to review by the Kammergericht (an appeal court on competition matters), with a further appeal to the Bundesgerichthof (Federal Appeal Court). Thus, unlike the United Kingdom but similar to the United States and the Common Market, the courts have contributed much to the clarification and development of competition law.

Agreements in restraint of competition

The GWB distinguishes between horizontal agreements in restraint of competition and vertical ones. Section 1 provides that:

> Agreement by enterprises or associations of enterprises for a common purpose, and resolutions of associations of enterprises are invalid in so far as they are apt to restrain competition and thereby affect the production or marketing or commercial goods or services.

Although the section applies in the main to horizontal agreements, it is possible for verticle agreements to fall within the section if the parties are promoting a common purpose. Since the 1973 amendment, agreements also include concerted practices, where firms act in conscious parallelism without a binding, or even a gentleman's agreement.

The Act does not contain any indication of the type of agreement or practices which are caught by the section. The scope of the legislation, as in the Common Market and United States law, depends therefore on the purpose and effect of the agreement, rather than on the legal form. As in the United States, the courts have held that certain agreements, such as price fixing, are as a matter of law treated as being harmful to competition, and that, therefore, there is no need for the Kartellamt to consider their purpose or effect.

Certain types of cartels are permitted by sections 2–8 of the GWB. There are four different degrees of exemptions from section 1. Some cartels are allowed on mere notification to the cartel authorities, and include those entered into for the adoption of uniform standards and types, and export cartels. A second category is allowed if the cartel authorities do not disapprove of them within 3 months of notification. The more important ones are certain specialization agreements if it can be shown that unit costs will be reduced; co-operation agreements between small businesses; and agreements relating to the adoption of general conditions of business. A third group of cartels is allowed provided they are expressly authorized by the cartel authorities, including rationalization agreements not otherwise allowed, and 'crisis cartels', formed to overcome some deep-seated problem in a branch of the economy. Finally, the Federal Minister for the Economy has the power to authorize cartels in the interests of the national economy and the general public.

Vertical agreements are treated separately from cartels. Restrictions relating to the terms of the agreement are unlawful under section 15, to the extent that they restrict the freedom of a person to determine the conditions at which he deals with others. This covers resale price maintenance agreements and any other agreement which imposes restrictions on resale such as most favourable treatment clauses. Unlike United Kingdom law, it will also cover agreements to sell at maximum prices. Under section 16, the prices of books and other publications can be fixed, and manufacturers of branded goods can make a recommendation as to the resale price, though the Kartellamt can issue prohibition orders in the case of abuse, e.g. where consumers may be misled.

Agreements which restrict a person's freedom to choose with whom to deal, such as exclusive distribution contracts, are not expressly prohibited, but are subject to review by the Kartellamt. It has the power to declare such agreements void if the restraints substantially restrict competition. Patent licensing agreements are allowed, provided that the restriction on competition is not greater than is required to protect the patent.

Dominant positions

Section 22 of the GWB provides a general system of control over anti-competitive behaviour by firms with market power, though market power or dominance in itself is not unlawful. The aim is to prevent any abuse of a dominant position within the market. Therefore there must be a dominant position in the relevant market, and this position must be abused.

Market dominance can be established either by reference to the conduct of firms or to the structure of the industry. There are a number of definitions of market dominance in the legislation. The original legislation defines market dominance as the situation where 'a seller or buyer of . . . goods or commercial services . . . has no competitors or is not exposed to substantial competition'. This was added to by the 1973 amendment which provides that market dominance exists if a firm has a superior market position in relation to competitors, with particular regard being paid to its market share, access to markets, financial strength and the ability to erect barriers to entry into the market. The legislation also treats as being market dominant two or more firms who conduct their businesses in such a way that there is no real competition between them, and taken together they otherwise satisfy the criteria for market dominance, a stance which is similar to the complex monopoly situation in United Kingdom law.

In relation to structure, market dominance is presumed in a number of cases. Where one firm has one-third, two or three firms together one-half, and up to five firms two-thirds of the relevant market, a dominant position is taken to exist. These presumptions do not apply in the case of small or medium sized firms which have less than a stated annual turnover.

The Act does not define abuse, which is therefore left to the interpretation of the Kartellamt and Kammergericht. It is clear that in Germany, abuse of a dominant position is a legal concept, and the cartel authorities cannot implement economic policy as under the monopolies legislation in the United Kingdom. However, the 1980 amendment did specify three types of conduct where a dominant enterprise is deemed to have abused its dominant position. These are:

(a) where it unjustifiably obstructs other firms from entering the market;
(b) where it quotes prices and conditions different from

those which it would have obtained in a competitive market;
(c)   where it quotes prices or conditions in one market less favourable than those which it quotes in comparable markets.

The Act also contains provisions prohibiting certain anti-competitive behaviour. It is unlawful for a firm in a dominant position to engage in conduct which would be prohibited if it were the subject of a cartel agreement. Also prohibited are boycotts requiring a customer to stop dealing with a particular firm and unreasonable discrimination against other enterprises, when practised by firms in a dominant or relatively strong market position.

Enforcement

Enforcement is almost entirely in the hands of the Bundeskartellamt, though each Länder or state has a limited role in enforcement through their own Kartellamt. The Kartellamt has the power to impose fines on firms for breaches of the legislation, and these can amount up to three time the excess receipts derived from operation of the unlawful practices. The Kartellamt can also issue an injunction to prevent the operation of an unlawful agreement, and can issue an order prohibiting an enterprise from abusing a dominant market position. The decisions of the Kartellamt are subject to an appeal to the Kammergericht, and ultimately, on point of law, to the Bundesgerichthof.

The law also makes provision for the enforcement of the competition rules by private action for damages or an injunction by any person who has suffered harm through an infringement of the legislation, provided it can be shown that the provision infringed is designed to protect a particular group of people of whom he is one. However, it is not entirely clear as to which provisions are protective ones. It seems clear that the prohibition of boycotts and discriminatory practices are protective, but it is more doubtful in other cases, though the prohibition on cartels is probably a protective provision.

The claim for damages requires proof of fault, but an injunction can be obtained to restrain further infringements irrespective of the fault of the defendant. Very few civil cases are in fact brought, probably due to the difficulties of showing, first of all, that it is a protective provision that has been breached, and secondly, if so, the plaintiff was a person the Act was intended to protect. Unlike in the United States, but similar to the position in the United Kingdom, most enforcement is through administrative action.

Mergers

Germany has the most comprehensive, and probably the most complex, merger control in the world. Merger controls were first established by the 1973 amendment to the GWB, and have since been tightened.

Mergers are very widely defined in the Act, and include the acquisition of shares of varying percentages depending on size; interlocking directors; control contracts, that is where one company exercises control over another through contract; and any other link between firms that could subject one firm to the dominance of another.

If a merger is significant to competition it must be notified to the Kartellamt. This exists in three situations. They are:

(1)   if the merger creates or increases a market share of more than 20 per cent in a particular market;
(2)   if a participating firm has a market share of 20 per cent or more in another market;
(3)   if a participating firm has 100,000 employees or a turnover of DM500 million.

Advance notice of a merger must be given, and clearance received from the Kartellamt, if two or more of the parties to the proposed merger has a turnover of DM1 billion, or a single enterprise has a turnover of DM2 billion.

At one time, mergers involving a small firm with a turnover of DM50 million or less were exempt from the merger control. However, abuse of these exemptions by large firms buying up small firms led to the tightening of the exemption provisions in the 1980 amendment. They are now inapplicable where a firm with a turnover exceeding DM1 billion acquires a firm with a turnover of more than DM4 million.

The Kartellamt has the power to prohibit a merger if it creates or strengthens a dominant market position, unless the parties to the merger can show that the merger promotes competition in the market to a degree sufficient to outweigh the dominant position. It is presumed that a position of market dominance will ensue if a firm with a turnover of DM2 billion merges with a smaller enterprise, and the market is one in which small firms predominate, or the merger is between firms with a turnover of DM12 billion, and two of the participants each have a turnover of DM1 billion. Where a merger has already taken place, the Kartellamt can order the participants to unscramble it.

There is the right of appeal against the prohibition of a merger, not only to the Kammergericht, but also to the Federal Minister for the Economy. He can overrule the Kartellamt on the grounds that the anti-competitive effects of the merger are outweighed by the overall economic advantages, or is justified by an overriding public interest. In this way, some form of political control is maintained over mergers, but generally, unlike the United Kingdom, merger control is legal rather than political.

One case where the minister overruled the Kammergericht was the Veba-Gelsenberg merger in 1974. This was an attempt to establish a German oil company able to compete in a market dominated by overseas multinationals. The merger was initially prohibited, but the minister allowed the merger to proceed on the ground of overriding public interest.

Contrast with United Kingdom law

As the brief outline of the competition laws and policies of the United States and West Germany show, there are a wide variety of ways of controlling various anti-competitive practices. The United Kingdom approach differs in two important respects from both these countries, and indeed from those of most other countries, as well as from the Common Market approach. The first is that United Kingdom law is said to be based on the legal form specified in the legislation, as opposed to the system of control based on the purpose of effect of restricting competition. Secondly, the United Kingdom is almost unique in basing its control on civil sanctions and administrative or political action, rather than imposing penal sanctions.

Form and effect

The United Kingdom approach, as has been seen, uses a form based approach, although some movement has recently been made towards an effects based approach in the Competition Act in relation to the practices of a single firm which have the purpose or effect of restricting, distorting or preventing competition. The form based approach is especially marked in respect of restrictive trading agreements where only those which comply with a particular form have to be registered. Agreements which restrict competition, but do not fall within the form required by the legislation are perfectly valid, irrespective of their effect on competition. Conversely, if an agreement falls within the form prescribed, then it has to be registered even if the effects on competition are non-existent.

The approach in most other countries is based on purpose and effect. As discussed above, the Sherman Act in the United States prohibits all agreements which are in restraint of commerce, while in West Germany, the GWB prohibits agreements and practices which have the effect of restraining competition. Similar results are achieved in France and Japan, and even those countries with registration systems like the United Kingdom, as in Denmark, usually exclude from registration, agreements which do not have anti-competitive effect.

In practice, however, the distinction is not quite so clear cut. In the United Kingdom, the form based approach is only important in relation to initial registration. The subsequent evaluation by the Director and Court is almost entirely concerned with the effects of the agreement, though the 'gateway' criteria impose some limitation. Where the effects based approach is used, it is common to exclude certain forms of agreement, as in West Germany. The effects doctrine is thus modified by provisions that agreements which comply with a certain form are allowed.

It is also becoming common for many countries to prescribe that some agreements are always 'anticompetitive', whether they have an adverse effect on competition or not. In the United States, certain practices such as price-fixing and market sharing are illegal *per se*, as is price-fixing in Germany. Although the approach may be different, the end result is often the same, that is the prohibition, with exceptions, of agreements and other practices which have an adverse effect on competition.

Penalties and sanctions

The United Kingdom approach also differs in relation to the sanctions for breach of the rules. Penalties cannot be imposed for infringements of the regulations, unless a court order is obtained and the order is broken, when contempt proceedings can be brought. The United Kingdom procedure can restrain future conduct, but cannot punish for past action.

This is in contrast with both the United States and West Germany, as has been seen. In the United States violation of the Sherman Act is a criminal offence, while in West Germany the Kartellamt has substantial powers to impose fines. In relation to mergers, although the competition authorities in the United Kingdom have the duty to keep mergers under review, and certain investigative powers exist, the power to forbid a merger is kept firmly within the political sphere, which is in direct contrast with the United States and Germany, where although the government retain some control, merger control is legal and administrative.

Bibliography

Bailey, E. E. (1982), Foreword to Baumol, W. J., Panzar, J. C. and Willig, R. D., *Contestable Markets and the Theory of Industry Structure* (New York: Harcourt Brace Jovanovich).

Baumol, W. J., Panzar, J. C. and Willig, R. D. (1982) *Contestable Markets and the Theory of Industry Structure* (New York: Harcourt Brace Jovanovich).

Bellamy, C. W., and Child, D. (1978), *Common Market Law of Competition* (London: Sweet & Maxwell).

Borrie, G. (1980), 'The relationship between U.K. and EEC Competition Law and Policies', in F. M. Rowe, F. G. Jacobs and M. R. Joelson (eds), *Enterprise Law of the 80's* (New York: ABA Press).

Clarke, R., Davies, S., and Waterson, M. (1984), 'The profitability–concentration relation: market power or efficiency?', *Journal of Industrial Economics*, vol. 32, pp. 435–50.

Clarke, J. M. (1940), 'Toward a concept of workable competition', *American Economic Review*, vol. 30, pp. 241–56.

Cowling, K. and Mueller, D. C. (1978), 'The social costs of monopoly power', *Economic Journal*, vol. 88, pp. 724–48.

Cunningham, J. P. (1981), *The Competition Act 1980* (London: Sweet & Maxwell).

Cunningham, J. P. (1974), *The Fair Trading Act 1973* (London: Sweet & Maxwell).

Demsetz, H. (1969), 'Information and efficiency: another viewpoint', *Journal of Law and Economic*, vol. 12, pp. 1–22.

Demsetz, H. (1973), 'Industry structure, market rivalry and public policy', *Journal of Law and Economics*, vol. 16, pp. 1–10.

Demsetz, H. (1974), 'Two systems of belief about monopoly', in H. J. Goldschmid (ed.), *Industrial Concentration: The New Learning* (Boston: Little Brown), pp. 164–184.

Fama, E. F. (1980), 'Agency problems and the theory of the firm', *Journal of Political Economy*, vol. 88, pp. 272–84.

Forrester, I., and Norall, C. (1984), 'How competition law is and could be applied', *Common Market Law Review*, vol. 21, no. 1, pp. 11–51.

Hansard, vol. 406, HL Deb., 20 February 1980, vol. 64.

Harberger, A. C. (1954), 'Monopoly and resource allocation', *American Economic Review, Proceedings*, vol. 44, pp. 73–87.

Hay, D. A. and Morris, D. J. (1979), *Industrial Economics: Theory and Evidence* (Oxford: OUP).

Holl, P. (1977), 'Control type and the market for corporate control in large US corporations', *Journal of Industrial Economics*, vol. 25, pp. 259–73.

Horn, N., Kotz, H., and Leser, H. G. (1982), *German Private and Commercial Law* (Oxford: Clarendon).

Kerse, C. S. (1981), *EEC Antitrust procedure* (London: European Law Centre).

Kon. S. (1982), 'Article 85, para. 3: a case for application by national courts', *Common Market Law Review*, vol. 19, no. 4, pp. 541–61.

Korah, V. (1975), *Competition Law of Britain and the Common Market*, 2nd Ed. (London: Paul Elek).

Korah, V. (1978), *An Introductory Guide to EEC Competition Law and Practice* (Oxford: ESC).

Koutsoyannis, A. (1975), *Modern Microeconomics* (London: Macmillan).

Lasok, D. (1980), *The Law of the Economy in the European Communities* (London: Butterworth).

Lasok, D., and Bridge, J. W. (1982), *An Introduction of the Law and Institutions of the European Communities*, 2nd Ed. (London: Butterworth).

Lee, N. (1979), 'Performance measurement', in P. J. Devine, N. Lee, R. M. Jones and W. J. Tyson (ed.), *An Introduction to Industrial Economics* (London: Allen & Unwin), pp. 300–27.

Leisner, H. (1978), *A Review of Monopolies and Mergers Policy* (London: HMSO).

Leisner, H. (1979), *A Review of Restrictive Trade Practices Policy* (London: HMSO).

Littlechild, S. C. (1981), 'Misleading calculations of the social costs of monopoly power', *Economic Journal*, vol. 91, pp. 348–63.

McNulty, P. J. (1967) 'A note on the history of perfect competition', *Journal of Political Economy*, vol. 75, pp. 173–87.

Mason, E. S. (1937), 'Monopoly in law and economics', *Yale Law Journal*, p. 49.

Phillips, A. (1976), 'A critique of empirical studies of relations between market structure and profitability', *Journal of Industrial Economics*, vol. 24, pp. 241–9.

Posner, R. A. (1975), 'The social costs of monopoly and regulation', *Journal of Political Economy*, vol. 83, pp. 807–27.

Reekie, W. D. (1979), *Industry, Prices and Markets* (Oxford: Philip Allan).

Smith, P., and Swann, D. (1979), *Protecting the Consumer* (Oxford: Martin Robertson).

Steindorff, E. (1983), 'Article 85, para. 3: no case for application by national courts', *Common Market Law Review*, vol. 20, no. 2, pp. 125–30.

Stigler, G. (1956), 'Report on antitrust policy-discussion', *American Economic Review*, p. 505.

Thompson, G. C., and Brady, G. P. (1979), *Anti-Trust Fundamentals* (St. Paul, Minn: West).

Webb, M. G. (1976), *Pricing Policies for Public Enterprises* (London: Macmillan).

Whish, R. P. (1982), 'EEC competition law in national courts', *New Law Journal*, September 9, pp. 855–56.

Index